EDINBURGH WALKS

Volume Two
The Pentlands and The Lothians

CAMPBELL BROWN & STEVEN WIGGINS

Maps
Simon Manfield

Photographs & Illustrations
Steven Wiggins

First Published 1990
by B+W Publishing
Edinburgh
Printed in Scotland
at Meigle Printers Ltd
Galashiels
© Campbell Brown & Steven Wiggins
ISBN 0 9515151 3 6

Other titles available

Edinburgh Walks Volume One

ISBN 0 9515151 0 1

Glasgow Walks

ISBN 0 9515151 1 X

B+W Publishing 7 Sciennes Edinburgh EH9 1NH

Contents

12 pages of photographs between pages 59 & 60

Authors Note

Throughout the text you will find a series of numbers. These relate directly to the numbers on the maps and will enable you to see at a glance exactly where the information relevant to any point of interest on the walk is to be found. We have also included **OS map references** to help you locate the start of every walk.

Details of suitable buses can be obtained from Eastern Scottish at St Andrew Square 031-556 8464 and LRT 031-220 4111.

Acknowledgements
We would like to thank:
The Desktop Publishing Centre (031-558 3136)
The Graphics Company (031-557 8675)
Simon "Maps" Manfield for his unstinting cartography

b+w

Introduction

The main thing to remember when walking in the countryside is to use common sense, both in the equipment you take with you and the way you treat the environment. Much of the land you pass through is privately owned farmland and a few basic rules should be followed:

- keep to rights of way whenever possible
- avoid fields under cultivation
- take particular care during the grouse shooting season from August to October
- avoid creating disturbances during the lambing season from April to June, and take special care to ensure that dogs are kept under control
- if in doubt about any of the above, contact the **Ranger Advice Centres** at Hillend **(031-445-3383)** or Flotterstone **(71-77879).**

We have made every effort to ensure that the information in this book is accurate. However, the inclusion of a walk in this guide does not necessarily guarantee access and it is up to the walker, if in doubt, to check that the route is still open. Because the countryside is not a static environment, conditions may well alter as time goes on, but intelligent use of the recommended maps should overcome any such difficulties.

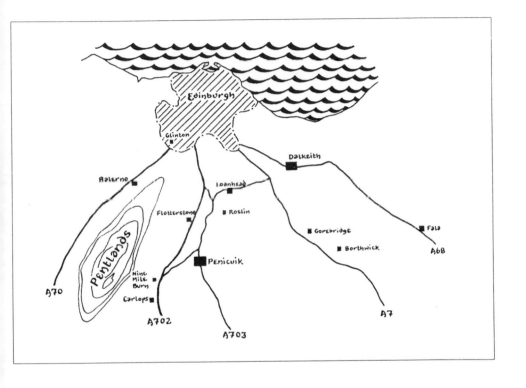

Midlothian

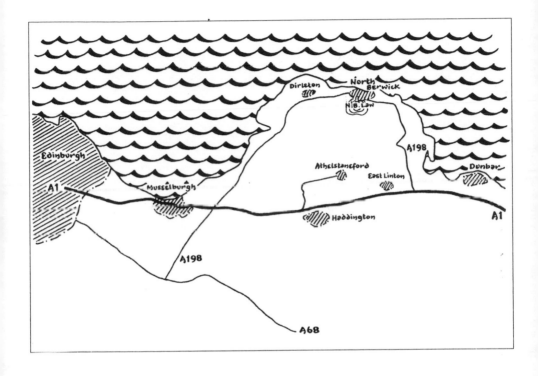

East Lothian

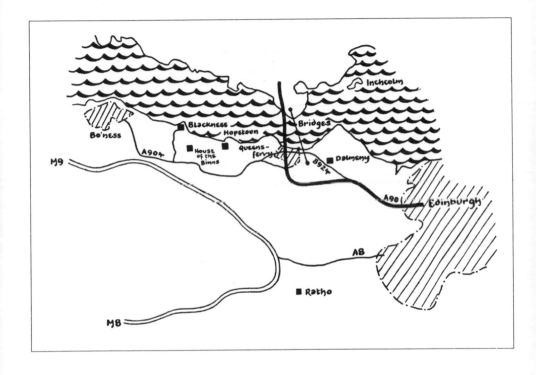

West Lothian

...in solitary hills and morasses,
haunted only by the so-called
mountain wanderers, the
dragoons that came in chase of
them, the women that wept on
their dead bodies, and the wild
birds of the moorland that have
cried there since the beginning. It
is a land of many rainclouds, a land
of much mute history, written
there in prehistoric symbols.

Heathercat by
Robert Louis Stevenson

1
Swanston Village to the Pentlands

Thatched Village
Robert Louis Stevenson
Edwin Muir
Caerketton and Allermuir Hills
The Covenanters

Recommended Maps
Bartholomew Pentland Hills Walking Map,
Ordnance Survey Landranger Map 66

**Distance approx 3 miles, depending
on route chosen.**

Directions to Start
Follow the main A702 through Morningside
and continue to the end of Comiston Road
at Fairmilehead. Turn right at the traffic lights
and then left into Swanston Road. Continue
along to the village and park in the car park.

Starting Point
**From the car park (1), turn right and
walk up to Swanston Village (2)**

OS Map Ref 240674

Swanston Village is a collection of delightful, white, thatched cottages nestling in a valley at the foot of Caerketton Hill. It was a source of inspiration for Edwin Muir, the poet, novelist, essayist and teacher. At the top of the slope, the bench which overlooks the village bears the inscription

"given by his friends to the village of Swanston where the poet liked to linger and meditate".

Walk through the gate at the top of the village and turn right down the slope and across to the golf course. The house in the trees is **Swanston Cottage (3).**

In 1867, **Robert Louis Stevenson**'s father, an engineer and lighthouse builder, took over the lease on Swanston Cottage, less of a cottage than a small mansion house, so that his family could enjoy the peace and tranquility of the Pentland countryside at the weekends and for holidays. The main family home was at 17 Heriot Row, in the heart of the bustling New Town, and although the young Stevenson had a pleasant view of Queen Street Gardens to inspire him, this never had the same attraction as Swanston, where the hills with their historical associations fired his imagination. His first serious work as a writer was done here as a student, and was based on one of his favourite stories, the **Battle of Rullion Green**, where in 1666 a small, ill equipped army of Covenanters faced up to an army three times its size **(see Walk 2)**.

Stevenson's affinity with Swanston remained to the end of his life, and his unfinished novel St Ives, written in Samoa, has a long description of the cottage. Unable to finish St Ives, he worked instead on his final novel *The Weir of Hermiston*. The last prophetic words he wrote, before his death from a cerebral haemorrage on the 3rd December 1894, were **"a wilful convulsion of brute nature....."**.

Walk back to the path and up through the golf course. Follow the arrow on the post and ahead is the walk up to the hills. Continue up the hill past the crags of Byreside Hill and round to the top of **Allermuir Hill (1617 ft)**. *From here walk*

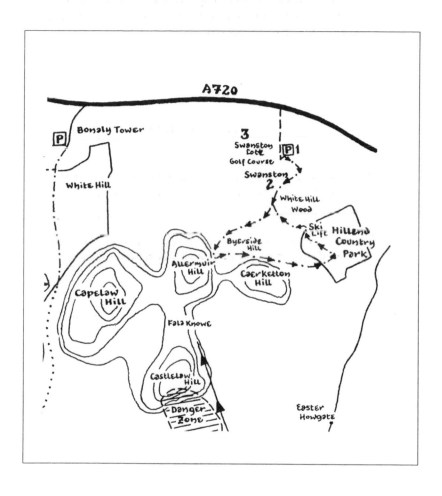

across to **Caerketton Hill (1550 ft)** *and down into the Hillend Country Park, or straight back to Swanston by keeping the ski-lift and White Hill Wood below you.*

Alternative routes:

1 The easy route: turn left at the bottom of Caerketton Hill and walk across to the ski-lift and down into Hillend Country Park.

2 Walk south from Allermuir Hill, across Fala Knowe and Castlelaw Hill to **Castlelaw Hill Fort and Souterrain** (see Walk 3).

The cottage was a little quaint place of
rough-cast gables and grey roofs. It had
the air of a rambling infinitesimal cathedral,
the body of it rising in the midst of two
storeys high, with a steep-pitched roof, and
sending out upon all hands (as it were
chapter-houses, chapels and transepts) one-
storeyed and dwarfish projections. To add
to the appearance it was grotesquely
decorated with crockets and gargoyles,
ravished from some mediaeval church. The
place seemed hidden away, being not only
concealed in the trees of the garden, but,
on the side on which I approached it,
buried as high as the eaves by the rising of
the ground.

From *St Ives* by **Robert Louis Stevenson**

2
Rullion Green and the Martyrs Tomb

Glencorse Old Church
Robert Louis Stevenson
Covenanters Battlefield
Martyrs Tomb

Recommended Maps
Bartholomew Pentland Hills or Ordnance Survey
Landranger 66

Walking Distance 3 miles

Directions to Start
A702 from Edinburgh to Flotterstone.
Car Parking at Visitor Centre.

Starting Point
Flotterstone Inn (1)

OS Map Ref 234631

*Walk back to the main road and turn left. Continue to the
first road on the right. Walk down to Glencorse, about half a
mile on the left.*

Glencorse Old Church (2) is just past the entrance to Glencorse
House, and up the small lane to the left. Unfortunately, this eerie ruin, with
its roofless chapel and 17th century tombstones is on private ground and
can only be viewed through the locked gates. The house is also private
property. Despite this, it is well worth pausing in this secluded spot to see
the typical 17th century memento mori, the hourglasses, skulls, cross-
bones and shovels.

**"Death
is not care it is
not pain but it is rest
and peace. Death
makes all our terrors vain
and bids our torments cease
This stone is for te mark the ground
Where Mary Simson lies
Lawful wife to John McKeen
Till death did close hir eyes"
16th July 1842, age 65**

The old church was one of Robert Louis Stevenson's favourite places. He
made use of it in his short story *The Body-Snatcher*, and he described it thus
to Sidney Colvin: "it is a little cruciform place, with a steep slate roof. The
small kirkyard is full of old gravestones; one of a Frenchman from
Dunkerque. I suppose he died prisoner in the military prison hard by; and
one, the most pathetic memorial I ever saw, a poor school slate in a
wooden frame, with the inscription cut into it evidently by the father's own
hand." Later, writing from Samoa, he asked a favour of Mr Crockett of
Glencorse: "I shall never take that walk by the Fisher's Tryst and
Glencorse. I shall never see Auld Reekie. I shall never set my foot again on
the heather. Do you know where the road crosses the burn under

Glencorse Church? Go there and say a prayer for me. See that it is a sunny day; I would like it to be Sunday; but that's not possible in the premises; and stand on the right bank just where the road goes down into the water, and shut your eyes; and if I don't appear to you!"

Walk back down the lane and turn right, and take the left fork towards Glencorse Mains. Continue through Glencorse Mains and continue on to the T-junction. Turn right and walk back up towards the A702. At the junction with the A702 turn left and walk up the hill, past the house on the left and on to the farm road on the right. This goes up to Rullion Green farm. Walk past the house, through the gate, and up in the woods to the left you will see the red railings of the Martyrs Tomb.

As Rullion Green is a working farm, it is important to ensure that no disturbance is caused, especially at lambing time, and it is advisable to seek permission from the farmer if you wish to visit the site.

The Martyrs Tomb (3) marks the site of the **Battle of Rullion Green**. It was here on the 28th of November 1666 that the covenanters under the command of Captain James Wallace met the government troops led by General Thomas Dalyell.

The **Pentland Rising** only lasted two weeks and it was 'the protest of downtrodden men against taskmasters whose cruelties had become intolerable'. Four covenanters, who had been hiding out close to Loch Ken in Galloway, became involved in a dispute between some of **Sir James Turner**'s troopers and an old man who refused to pay his fine for being absent from church. The troopers were threatening to roast him alive. This incensed the covenanters who drew swords and pistols and attacked the troopers, one of whom, Corporal George Deanes, was wounded. The rest of the soldiers were taken prisoner and the uprising began. The rising gathered momentum and with support from the local population the covenanters decided to march on Dumfries, with the intention of capturing Sir James Turner. With 180 men, about half of whom were well armed, they arrived at Dumfries on the 15th November. Turner was caught completely

8

"At length an occasion arose which threw the pair once more into a closer union. Mr K was again short of subjects... At the same time there came the news of a burial in the rustic graveyard of Glencorse. Time has little changed the place in question. It stood then, as now, upon a crossroad, out of call of human habitations, and buried fathom deep in the foliage of six cedar trees... The resurrection man – to use a by-name of the period – was not to be deterred by any of the sanctities of customary piety. It was part of his trade to despise and desecrate the scrolls and trumpets of old tombs, the paths worn by the feet of worshippers and mourners, and the offerings and the inscriptions of bereaved affection. To rustic neighbourhoods, where love is more than commonly tenacious, and where some bonds of blood or fellowship unite the entire society of a parish, the body-snatcher, far from being repelled by natural respect, was attracted by the ease and safety of the task. To bodies that had been laid in earth, in joyful expectation of a far different awakening, there came that hasty, lamp-lit, terror-haunted resurrection of the spade and mattock.

Somewhat as two vultures may swoop upon a dying lamb, Fettes and MacFarlane were to be let loose upon a grave in that quiet resting place. The wife of a farmer was to be rooted from her grave at midnight...the place beside her family was to be empty till the crack of doom; her innocent and almost venerable members to be exposed to that last curiosity of the anatomist."

The Body-Snatcher by Robert Louis Stevenson

unawares, and with a garrison of only 12 men, he was forced to surrender. Despite his reputation for persecuting the covenanters he was well treated by his captors; although he complained about the abominable length and tedium of the Grace said before meals. By now, an army of 2500 had left Edinburgh under the command of **General Thomas Dalyell**, Commander-in-Chief of the King's forces in Scotland (see House of the Binns, Walk 21), and had set off in pursuit of the rebels.

The covenanters were now being led by **Captain James Wallace**, who had fought for **Cromwell** in the English Civil War, and amongst his officers were three men who had fought alongside Dalyell at the Battle of Worcester in 1651: Major Learmont, Captain Arnott and Captain John Paton. The two armies finally met at Rullion Green in the late afternoon of the 28th November 1666. The fighting started around the burn and it was at this point that John Crookshank and Andrew McCormack, whose names appear on the Martyrs Tomb, were killed in hand to hand fighting. As darkness began to fall the sheer weight of numbers of the King's forces prevailed and the covenanters were chased from the field of battle. About fifty were killed and seventy were captured.

Towards the end of the battle, Dalyell saw his old comrade Captain Paton escaping across the burn and sent three cavalry troopers after him. Paton turned and fought, killed the first of them, and drove off the other two telling them "take my compliments to your master, and tell him that I cannot sup with him tonight." Captain Wallace also escaped and fled to Holland. Others were not so fortunate and many covenanters perished in the series of executions which followed. The Rising was over.

The Royalist's second-in-command was **General Drummond** who had served with Dalyell in Russia, and the following is an extract from Drummond's account of the Battle of Rullion Green as sent to the Earl of Rothes.

> "Wee pursued in the dark, killed all the foot and but for the night and steep hills had wholly destroyed them. Some prisoners are fitt for examples. I do not

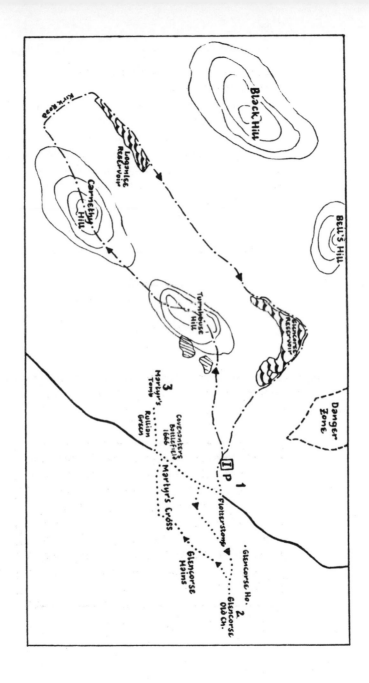

Black Hill

Bell's Hill

Kirk Road

Loganlee Reservoir

Carnethy Hill

Glencorse Reservoir

Turnhouse Hill

Danger Zone

3
Martyr's Tomb
Rullion Green

Covenanters
Battlefield
1666

Martyr's Cross

Glencorse Mains

P
1
Flotterstone

Glencorse Ho.

2
Glencorse
Old Ch.

11

know how many but I conjecture not above 140, for there was sound payment.

Our losse I cannot tell, but it is greater than many of their skins were worth, their number was about 15 or 1600 and would without doubt have encreased if God had not confounded their imaginacons and rebellious dispositions. Upon Monday the rebells swore the covenant at Lenrick and all to die in defence of it, most of these who led their troops were cashiered preachers.

Now I trust your grace is at ease. I am.

Yr grces
most obedient and most humble servt

W. Drummond.

The Martyrs Tomb itself, marking the place where many of those killed in the battle were buried, dates from the 1730's and bears the following inscriptions:

> "Here and nar to this plece, lyes the Reverend Mr John Crookshanks and Mr Andrew McCormock ministers of the Gospel and about 50 other true Covenanted Presbyterians who were killed in this place in their own inocent self defence and defence of the Covenanted work of Reformation by Thomas Dalyell of Bins upon the 28th November 1666." Rev 12.11

> "A cloud of witnesses lyes here,
> Who for Christ's interest did appear,
> For to restore true Liberty
> Overturned then by Tyranny
> And by Proud Prelates who did rage
> Against the Lord's own heritage.
> They sacrificed were for the Laws
> Of Christ their King, his noble cause.
> These heros fought with great renown
> By falling got the Martyrs crown"

Walk back to the A702, turn left and continue back to the Flotterstone Inn and the end of this walk ($^1/_2$ a mile).

3
Turnhouse Hill and the Reservoirs

Castlelaw Hill Fort
Rullion Green
Howlet's House
Thomas Telford
Information Centre

Recommended Maps
Bartholomew Pentlands Map

Distance 4 miles

Directions to Start
A702 south from Edinburgh to Flotterstone Inn

Starting Point
Information Centre car park (1)

OS Map Ref 632232

*From the car park, turn right and walk up the road following
the path left towards Turnhouse Hill. Cross the footbridge and
continue to the top of Turnhouse Hill (1636ft).*

Turnhouse Hill has commanding views

- to the north is **Glencorse Reservoir** with Castlelaw Hill (1595 ft) just
beyond.

- to the north east, the hill fort sits in the shadow of **Castlelaw Hill.** The
hill fort with its souterrain and earthwork fortifications dates from the
Iron Age and was a fairly substantial settlement ideally situated on an
igneous intrusion, and defended by a series of ramparts and ditches.
Originally there would only have been a single ditch and a timber pallisade,
but in the last centuries BC this was extended to form this rather more substantial barrier. It is thought that this type of Hill Fort would have originally
been simply a small farming community, but the inhabitants increasing need
to defend themselves and their livestock from attack, combined with the
excellent natural site, led to the development of the fort, the remains of
which can be seen today.

The function of souterrains, like this one and the even more elaborate one
at Crichton (OS 400619), is shrouded in mystery. They may have been used
for accomodation or storage, but it seems more plausible, given the
painstaking nature of their construction, that they served as some kind of
temple or burial site. **The Crichton Souterrain** is even more inacces-
sible, and has a distinctly mysterious atmosphere.

*Follow the path which descends about 200ft down the far side
of Turnhouse Hill before ascending 400ft to the cairn at the
summit of Carnethy Hill.*

This is how **Sir Walter Scott** described the scene
in his Journals:

"I think I never saw anything more beautiful than the ridge
of Carnethy against a clear frosty sky, with its peaks and
varied slopes. The hills glowed like purple amethyst; the sky
glowed topaz and vermilion colours. I never saw a finer
series than the Pentlands, considering it is neither rocky nor
highly elevated."

*Continue south west and turn north west, descending to the
end of Loganlee Reservoir. From here, follow the road round
Loganlee Reservoir, passing* **Howlet's House (2)** *on the
left on a small outcrop about half way along the reservoir.*

This ruin is thought to be the old manse house attached to the now submerged **St Catherines Chapel.** From here it is 1 mile north east along
the road to Glencorse Reservoir. Glencorse Reservoir was built between
1819 and 1822 at a cost of £145,000. The designer of the project was the
prolific Thomas Telford, and the work was completed by the Edinburgh
engineer James Jardine.

*Follow the road round the reservoir until the point where Kirk
Burn joins the reservoir from the north. At this point, if you
want to visit* **Castlelaw Hill Fort (3)**, *take the path that
follows the burn northwards before turning east around the
base of Castlelaw Hill to the Hill Fort.*

Before going through the gate at the fort, read the notice (partially
obscured by the grass at the bottom) about the army rifle range which
provides information about what signals are given before firing starts. The
range is down the hill to the left of the fort.

*If you do not want to walk to the Hill Fort, follow the road
round the reservoir which heads south east and back to the
car park and* **Starting Point (1)**, *about 1 mile further on.*

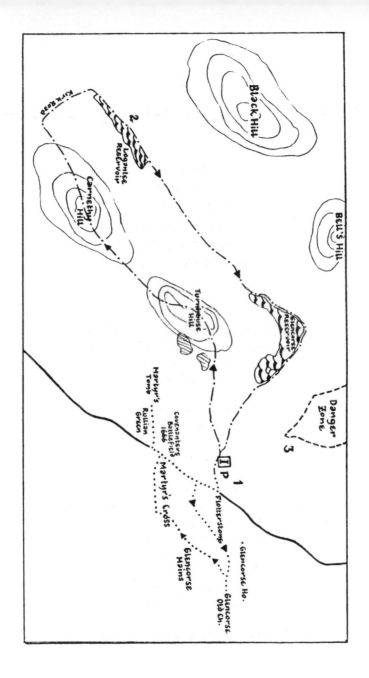

Black Hill

Bell's Hill

Kirk Road

2

Loganlee Reservoir

Carnethy Hill

Turnhouse Hill

Glencorse Reservoir

Danger Zone

3

Martyr's Tomb

Rullion Green

Covenanters Battlefield 1666

Martyr's Cross

Flotterstone

P

1

Glencorse Mains

Glencorse Ho.

Glencorse Old Ch.

4
Rosslyn Castle to Rosslyn Chapel

Rosslyn Castle
The Glen
Wallace's Cave
Rosslyn Chapel
Apprentice Pillar
The Old Rosslyn Inn

Opening Times
Rosslyn Castle is not open to the public.
Rosslyn Chapel open Easter-end of October, Mon-Sat
10am-5pm, Sun 12-5pm. Admission £1.50. Tearoom
and gift shop.

Recommended Map
Ordnance Survey Landranger 66

Distance 2 miles

Directions to Start
A701 south from Edinburgh, through Bilston, then turn
left onto B7003 and continue down into Roslin Glen.
The car park is on the left behind some industrial
buildings.

Starting Point
Roslin Glen car park (1)

OS Map Reference 273628

*Walk from the car park down through the trees towards the
river. Walk over the bridge and up towards the castle.
Continue up the hill and at the top of the steps the castle,
which is still privately owned, is on your right.*

Rosslyn Castle (2) towers above the valley of the North Esk. Originally
constructed at the start of the 14th century it was the ancestral home of
the St Clairs of Rosslyn, one of whom, Sir William, Prince of Orkney, began
the construction of the magnificent **Gothic Chapel**. In his time, the family
was immensely powerful, and even such important figures as the Lords of
Dirleton and Borthwick looked to him for leadership. The power of the St
Clair's was based on a long association with the Kings of Scotland which
had culminated in an earlier Sir William's participation in the **Battle of
Bannockburn** in 1314. However, the middle of the 15th century saw the
beginning of a series of misfortunes which led to the gradual decline of both
the castle and the influence of the St Clairs. In 1447 Edward St Clair apparently came upon a large number of rats while out hunting. One of them was
old, blind and carried a straw in its mouth. This was taken to be an evil
omen, and so it proved. Within days a serious fire had destroyed a large
section of Rosslyn Castle. Further misfortune followed a century later
when the castle was burned again during Henry VIII's **Rough Wooing** of
Mary Queen of Scots, whom he considered an ideal match for his son
Edward, Prince of Wales. Rosslyn Castle was not the only victim of Henry's
aggression, his army also sacked and burned Edinburgh and the Borders.
Along with many of the great castles of the Lothians, 1650 was to prove
a fateful year for Rosslyn. It took only one week for the artillery of
Cromwell's troops, led by General Monk, to batter Rosslyn and its garrison
of twenty five into submission, at the same time reducing much of the castle
to rubble. The castle's great days were over, and by the end of the 18th
century it was an abandoned ruin.

> **Oh, Roslin! Time, war, flood and fire,
> Have made your glories star by star expire.**
> Byron

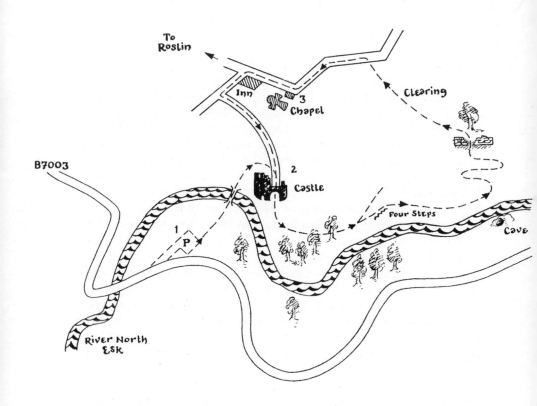

To
Roslin

Inn

3
Chapel

Clearing

B7003

2
Castle

Four Steps

Cave

1

P

River North
Esk

Today the ruined castle with its massive walls and vertiginous drawbridge still dominates the glen, occupying as it does one of the best natural defensive sites in the Lothians. Above the door of the only remaining habitable section of the castle are the initials of Sir William St Clair - **SWS 1622** - who died in 1650 and was the last Scottish knight to be buried in full armour.

> *Walk back down the steps and turn left and under the archway of the castle entrance, the drawbridge, and then left again at the sign towards Polton. This takes you into the dramatic **Roslin Glen** and onto the footpath beside the river. One of the best views of the castle is about 400 yards on, just before the path forks.*
>
> *When you get to the fork in the path, turn right and walk down the four log steps and down to the great rock overlooking the gorge. Continue along the edge of the river where there are many caves secreted in the rocky cliffs on the opposite side. At some points, the path is quite narrow but there is an iron handrail for support.*
>
> *At the junction of the paths, turn left and walk up the winding path which takes you high above the river.*

Looking across the river you will see the entrance to one of the many caves that **William Wallace** is reputed to have frequented. If Wallace had indeed visited as many caves as he is associated with - every river valley and hillside seems to have its own "Wallace's Cave" - he would rarely have set foot inside a normal dwelling.

> *At the top of the path, walk between the two sections of broken wall and turn left at the tree. Bear slightly to the right, pass through the clearing and follow the path until it meets the road. Turn left and walk round the corner to the chapel.*

Rosslyn Chapel (3) was built in the 15th century by Sir William St Clair and was originally intended to be a much larger building. However, it was

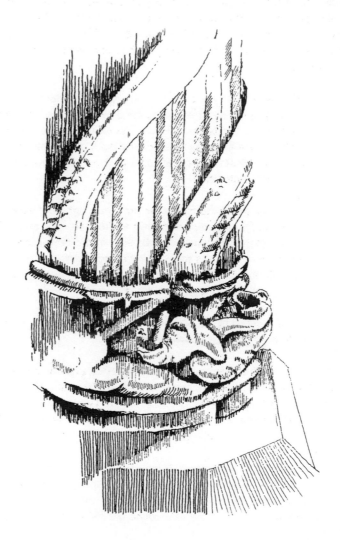

The Apprentice Pillar.

not finished in his lifetime and his heirs, not sharing his enthusiasm for this massive undertaking only managed to complete the roof. With its extravagant buttresses, stone vaulting and unique carving, Rosslyn Chapel is a Gothic masterpiece. The outside of the Chapel is notable for its flying buttresses, fearsome gargoyles and intricate doorway. Once inside the Chapel, the full extent of its creator's vision becomes apparent. The whole of the interior is a mass of **exquisite carving**, apparently carried out by continental master-masons, depicting all manner of biblical themes including the **'Dance of Death'** or the eternal struggle of mankind against the grim reaper.

The most famous feature of the Chapel is the **Apprentice Pillar**, with its beautiful carved dragons, near the stairway to the crypt. It is said that this pillar was carved by the master-mason's apprentice while he was absent. On his return, and seeing what his apprentice had achieved, the master-mason was consumed with jealousy and in a rage he murdered the apprentice in the Chapel. At the south west corner of the Chapel, high up on the wall, there is a carved head with a wound on its forehead, said to be a representation of the murdered apprentice. At the corresponding spot in the north west corner is a carving of the master-mason's head.

Also of interest is the dramatic stone roof with its **stars and roses,** and the crypt at the south east end fifteen feet below the level of the Chapel.

Turn left on leaving the Chapel and walk along to the Old Rosslyn Inn which dates from the 17th century.

Wordsworth, Scott, Johnson, Boswell and, in 1859, **the Prince of Wales** (later to be Edward VII) all visited the Inn.

Turn left at the Inn and walk down to the sign for Polton. Turn left here and walk down between the cemetery walls to Rosslyn Castle. Continue down the hill, across the bridge and back to the car park.

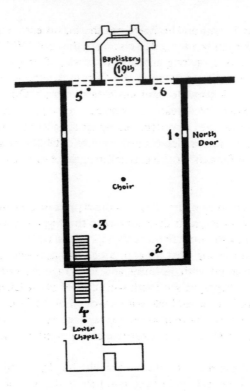

1	Main Door
2	Inverted Angel Carving
3	Apprentice Pillar
4	Lower Chapel
5	The Apprentice
6	The Mason

5
Colinton to
Malleny House Garden

Colinton Church and Mortsafe
Robert Louis Stevenson
The Water of Leith Walkway
Malleny House Garden
National Bonsai Collection of Scotland

Opening Times
Spylaw House is not open to the public
Malleny House Gardens open daily 10am-dusk
adult £1, children/OAP 50p, National Trust
members free; no dogs allowed

Recommended Map
Ordnance Survey Landranger 66

Distance approx 4 miles

Directions to Start
A702 to Holy Corner, turn right onto Colinton Road
and continue to the village itself. Drive down the hill
into the main street (Bridge Street) and turn right into
Spylaw Street. The starting point is just across the
bridge at the bottom of the hill.

Starting point
Colinton Church (1) in Dell Road.

OS Map Ref 216692

Colinton Church is built on an ancient religious site. There have been churches of one kind or another here since Pictish times but the first recorded date is 1248. That church was razed to the ground during the time of Henry VIII, by the Earl of Hertford's invasion force during the **Rough Wooing** of 1544. The present church dates from 1771, and among the tombstones in the churchyard are to be found some typical examples of Scots verse. The following example is near the MDCCLXXI stone set in the church wall:

> Death's a Dett
> To Nature Deeu
> I Have Paid it
> So Mon you

Near the door to the church is a **mortsafe**. Designed to enclose the ordinary wooden coffin, it was intended to defeat bodysnatchers. This is an extremely rare example of the lengths to which people were prepared to go in the 18th century to avoid the attentions of the bodysnatchers. These were people who stole freshly buried corpses to sell to anatomists for research purposes. Mortsafes were generally commissioned, not by an individual, but by a group of people. The reason for this was that once the body had decomposed the mortsafe would be exhumed and used again. Made of very thick sheets of iron and welded into a single solid block, it proved to be a formidable defence. Considering the use to which it was put, the example in Colinton churchyard is still in remarkably good condition.

Colinton Church's most notable minister was the Reverend Dr Lewis Balfour, who was **Robert Louis Stevenson's grandfather.** Stevenson described his grandfather as "a man of singular simplicity of nature; unemotional, and hating the display of what he felt; a lover of his life and innocent habits to the end. We children admired him; partly for his beautiful face and silver hair, for none more than children are concerned for beauty and, above all, for beauty in the old; partly for the solemn light in which we observed him once a week, the observed of all observers in the pulpit."

The young Stevenson often visited the manse with his mother, and it was at Colinton that the story of the Covenanters, who had camped here on their way to defeat at the Battle of Rullion Green in 1666, probably first came to his attention. Dr Balfour is buried in the churchyard, next to the massive tomb of James Gillespie of Spylaw at the back of the church.

> Walk out of the chuchyard and turn left. Walk across the
> bridge and up Spylaw Street to the path that leads past
> **Spylaw House (2)** and the start of the Water Of Leith
> Walkway.

Spylaw House was the home of **James Gillespie**, a tobacco and snuff manufacturer who, besides building this house, was a prominant philanthropist.

Malleny Garden Crest.

> Walk past the house and through the gap in the wall before
> the playground. Continue up the path to the left and across
> the bridge to the sign that points to Juniper Green. Follow this
> sign and the path leads all the way to Balerno and the
> Malleny House Garden.

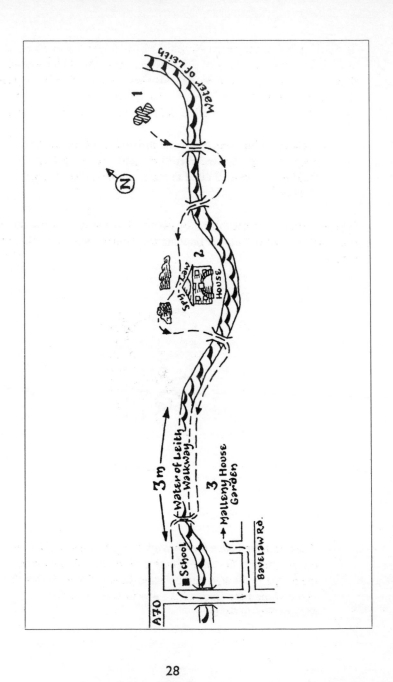

2

At the end of the path in Balerno, turn left at the main road, over the bridge and left into Bavelaw Road. On the left about 50 yards up the road is the entrance to Malleny House Gardens.

Malleny House Gardens (3) are under the care of the National Trust for Scotland. The garden is best viewed between June and October. Created by Commander Robert Rollo Gore-Browne Henderson and his wife, the garden was given to the National Trust in 1968 by Mrs Gore-Browne Henderson. The ornate gateway into the garden is a memorial to the Commander and features a spread eagle, the family crest, designed by W Schomberg Scott. The garden features a magnificent arrangement of yew trees, a topiary arch, a fine selection of roses and **the National Bonsai Collection of Scotland**. No doubt inspired by the nautical background of the garden's founder, the garden seats are all made from teak taken from naval vessels; such as HMS Birmingham, which took part in the Battle of Jutland in 1916.

Return to the start by the same route, or walk back along the main road.

6
Penicuik Railway Walk

Valleyfield Moument
Auchendinny Station
Firth Tunnel
Firth Viaduct
Roslin Glen

Recommended Map
Bartholomew Pentland Hills
Ordnance Survey Landranger 66

Distance 3 miles from Penicuik to Roslin

Tearoom
Rosslyn Chapel

Directions to Start
A701 south from Edinburgh to Penicuik. Turn left at St
Mungo's Church (derelict) which is at the apex of the
major bend in the main road in the centre of the town.
Continue down this B-road for about a mile to the
bridge over the river North Esk, and the small car park
is straight ahead on the other side of the bridge. There
is also a signpost indicating the direction of the walk.

Starting Point
Car Park (1)

OS Map Ref 245606

The official start of the railway walk is about a mile down the path to the right, but the only item of interest on this section is the **Valleyfield Monument** which sits on top of a wall at the edge of the overgrown site of an old mill. It dates from 1830 and was built close to where 309 French prisoners were buried during the **Napoleonic Wars**.

> "The mortal remains of 309 Prisoners
> of War who died in this neighbourhood
> between 21st March 1811 and 26th
> July 1814 are interred near this spot.
> Certain inhabitants of this parish,
> desiring to remember that all men
> are brethren caused this monument
> to be erected in the year 1830."

The use of the phrase 'certain inhabitants' suggests that despite the passing of 15 years, anti-French sentiments were still present in the local community and many would simply rather have forgotten these unfortunate prisoners.

> *From the car park, turn left and walk along the path, which
> follows the line of the old Penicuik to Bonnyrigg railway,
> constructed in 1872 by the Penicuik Railway Company.*

As with many of the smaller rural railway lines, the financial stringency of the 1960's and the **Beeching** Report led to its closure in 1967 - just one part of the wholesale destruction of much of the rail network. Had the line still been open today, it is easy to imagine how successful it could be with steam trains once more passing through its tunnels and over its viaducts. However, at least this one can still be enjoyed, unlike most of the lines that were cut by Beeching.

> *Walking along from the starting point, you pass under a small
> road bridge and then into open country and fields which are
> used primarily for grazing horses.*

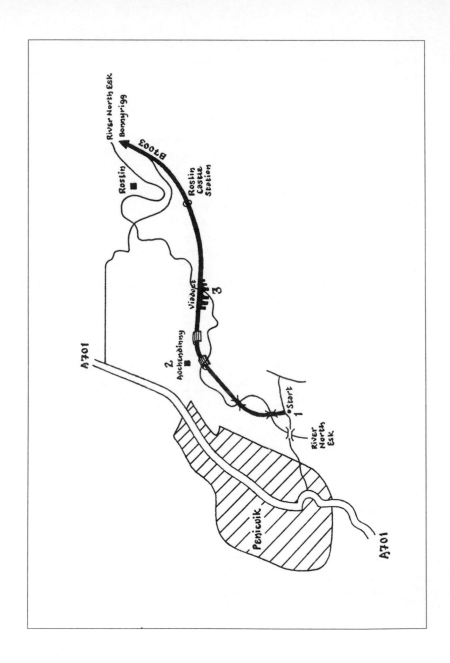

About $^3/_4$ mile further on you will come to the remains of **Auchendinny Station (2)**, with its overgrown platform still clearly visible. Close to this are two bridges, one built of iron which is particularly fine, and the other of stone, which lead into **Firth Tunnel.**

The combination of frequent horse traffic and the darkness in the tunnels mean that it is worth taking a torch to avoid treading in something unpleasant.

> *Continuing on along the path, you will walk past the Dalmore Paper Mill, and on to the next tunnel which leads onto the* **Firth Viaduct (3).**

The viaduct is in surprisingly good condition considering that it was designed by **Sir Thomas Bouch,** one of whose better known projects was the **Tay Bridge** which collapsed in 1879 as a train was passing over it. Bouch was originally commissioned to design a Forth Rail Bridge, but for obvious reasons his design was not accepted.

The viaduct has ten arches and is at its highest point above the River North Esk. Some of the most picturesque scenery in Midlothian can be seen from the viaduct. To the right is **Old Woodhouselee Castle**, where, as a young man, Sir Walter Scott practiced his art on attentive listeners with tales of ghosts and covenanters.

Just across the viaduct there used to be a tin tunnel which was intended to stop sparks from the trains igniting the gunpowder at the nearby gunpowder mill.

> *Walk on past the picnic site at* **Rosslyn Castle Station** *and on to where the railway joins the B7003. By turning left here you can walk down into Roslin Glen and the start of Walk 4. The final section of the railway walk to Bonnyrigg is less picturesque than the rest.*
>
> **Return to the start by the same route.**

7
Bavelaw Marsh and the Pentlands

The Red Moss Wildlife Reserve
Bavelaw Marsh
Threipmuir Reservoir
The Black Hill
Hare Hill
Logan Burn Waterfall
Howlet's House
Loganlee Reservoir
Glencorse Reservoir

4 walks in the Pentlands

(i) The Black Hill
(ii) Loganlee, Glencorse, Harlaw and Threipmuir
(iii) Hare Hill
(iv) Hare Hill, East Kip, West Kip and Scald Law

Recommended Map
Bartholomew Pentland Hills
Ordnance Survey Landranger 66

General information
No dogs allowed on Bavelaw Marsh Reserve
Bird hides available (key available from Balerno Post
Office or Pentland Hills Ranger Service, Hillend
Country Park - telephone 031 445 3383)

Bar
Marchbank Hotel

Directions to Start
A70 south west from Edinburgh to Balerno. Turn left
into Bridge Road and then left again into Bavelaw
Road. Continue up this road, past the entrance to the
Marchbank Hotel and bear left to the car park at
Bavelaw Marsh.

Starting Point
The Car Park at Bavelaw Marsh (1)

OS Map Reference 164638

Just beside the **car park (1)** is the **Red Moss Wildlife Reserve (2)**, a rare raised bog habitat. The feature is post-glacial, and was formed by a build up of layers of peat in the shallow basin left by ice action. There are very few similar locations in Britain, and the boggy pools are both fragile and dangerous. As you would expect, this rare habitat has some unusual flora and fauna: insectivorous sundew plants, ragged robin plants, orchids, sphagnum mosses, Emperor moths with their bright green markings and snipe with their characteristic springtime drumming sound made by the tail feathers of the male.

Walk up the road to Redford Bridge which crosses Threipmuir Reservoir and on your right is the Bavelaw Marsh Nature Reserve where one hundred and ten species of birds have been recorded, including heron, kestrel, sparrowhawk, moorhen, grebe and coot. Details of how to get into the hide are given above.

Continue walking up the tree lined avenue, and at the top there are four options for Pentland walks.

(i) The Black Hill - 1637 ft - OS ref 189632

- walk and steep hill climb

Distance approx 3 miles

From the top of the tree lined avenue, turn left and walk round past Bavelaw Castle, which is almost completely screened by trees and can only be seen from the Black Hill. Over the stile at the top of the road, the path to the left is obvious. Continue down the path to the second stile where the aptly named Black Hill towers above. There is a path which climbs rapidly up to the left and this is the best route to the top of the hill.

Alternatively, if you keep to the path there is a fairly easy walk to the Logan Burn waterfall and rock pools where there is an excellent place to picnic underneath the dramatic crags.

(ii) Loganlee, Glencorse, Harlaw and Threipmuir

Distance approx 8 miles

Following the same route as (i), the path continues round the Black Hill and down to Loganlee Reservoir. On the left, about half way down the reservoir is Howlet's House, all that remains of the manse of St Catherine's Chapel.

Continue walking down the road and turn left at the apex of Glencorse Reservoir. This path takes you along the Maiden's Cleuch between Harbour Hill and Bell's Hill and down to Harlaw Reservoir.

Turn left and walk down the side of Harlaw Reservoir, past Threipmuir Reservoir and back to the car park at Bavelaw Marsh.

(iii) Hare Hill - 1473 ft - OS ref 172620

- gentle walk and climb

Distance 3 miles

At the top of the tree lined avenue, turn right and follow the path round to the bottom of the hill. From the post at 1322 ft it is only another 150 ft to the summit of Hare Hill.

From the top of Hare Hill, King's Hill is to the left. This is where **Robert the Bruce** is said to have watched the hounds of Sir William St Clair

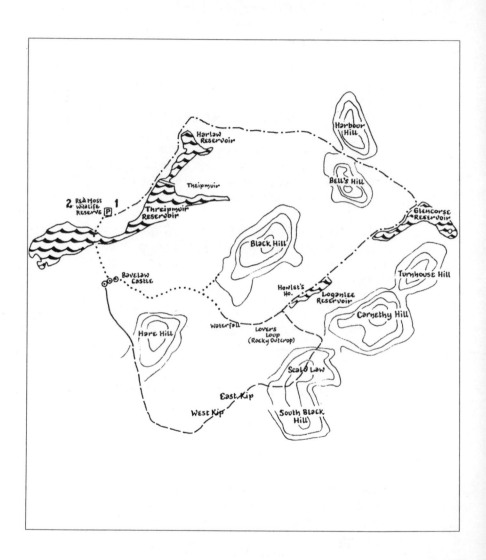

chasing a white deer. The king had mentioned to Sir William that he had never been able to catch the deer, at which point Sir William wagered his head that his dogs could do so before it reached the burn. The king accepted the rash bet and the hounds stopped the unfortunate animal just before the water. Delighted with the bet, the King granted Sir William the Forest of Pentland, and the relieved knight founded the now submerged **Chapel of St Catherines** at Glencorse to give thanks for his life.

(iv) Hare Hill to West Kip (1806ft), East Kip(1737ft) and Scald Law (1899ft)

- long walk with some steep climbs

Distance approx 7 miles

Following the same route as in (iii), continue along the path beside Hare Hill, across the Kitchen Moss and up to the 1500 ft post. At this point the path splits into four. Take the left path and continue up West Kip, over the slightly lower East Kip and finally Scald Law, the highest hill in the vicinity at 1899 ft. Walk down from Scald Law to the next junction of paths and turn left on to the Kirk Road.

At the T-junction at The Howe, the shortest way back to the starting point is to turn left. It is about 2 miles of easy walking back to the car park.

Alternatively, turn right and follow the road down beside the reservoirs and down the Maiden's Cleuch as described in section (ii). This increases the length of the walk to about 10 miles.

8
Borthwick Castle to Crichton Castle

Borthwick Church
Borthwick Castle
The Waverley Line
Crichton Castle
Crichton Church

Souterrain, an ancient and mysterious diversion at OS 400619. Take a torch.

Opening times
Borthwick Castle not open to the public, now an hotel.
Borthwick Church - key available from the old school-house, on the ledge in the porch. Please do not disturb the owners.
Crichton Castle open: summer Mon-Sat 9.30-7pm, Sun 2-7; winter only open at weekends

Recommended Maps
Ordnance survey Landranger 66

Directions to start
A7 south from Edinburgh past Gorebridge and left at North Middleton. Continue for one mile and Borthwick church is on your right.

Starting Point
Borthwick Church (1)

OS Map reference 369597

A church has stood on this spot since the 12th century, although the present one only dates from the 1860's. The original church was virtually destroyed by fire in 1775, and a new church was constructed near the present gates in 1778. This was a far less substantial building which by the middle of the 19th century could no longer accomodate the growing congregation. At this point **David Kidd**, inventor of the gummed envelope and owner of the Inveresk paper mill, offered to pay for a new church which was to be dedicated to the memory of his parents. Designed with a view to incorporating the remains of the original 12th century church, the new church, with its fine steeple, was completed in 1864.

As you enter the church take note of the interesting **carved heads** on either side of the door. Once inside the church the most interesting feature is undoubtedly the elaborate **15th century effigies**, reputed to depict the first Lord and Lady Borthwick. Although recently renovated, the effigies were originally far more ornate; gilded and painted in typical 15th century style.

The Borthwick family enjoyed a long association with the Scottish Crown - Sir William Borthwick twice acted as hostage for James I, the second Lord Borthwick was the head of James III's household, and the third Lord - James IV's falconer - died with his king at the battle of Flodden in 1513.

Outside, the churchyard is particularly pleasant, with its terrace sweeping down towards the river.

> *Walk back to the church gate and turn right at the information board. Continue down into the field and you will see the twin towers of Borthwick Castle.*

Borthwick Castle (2) is one of the best preserved tower houses in Scotland, unfortunately it is not open to the public as it is now an hotel. Over 100ft tall and with massive stone walls, Borthwick was a formidable fortress until the arrival of **General Monk's artillery** in 1650. The 10th Lord Borthwick had the good sense to surrender before much damage had been done, but the castle walls still bear the scars of the Cromwellian assault.

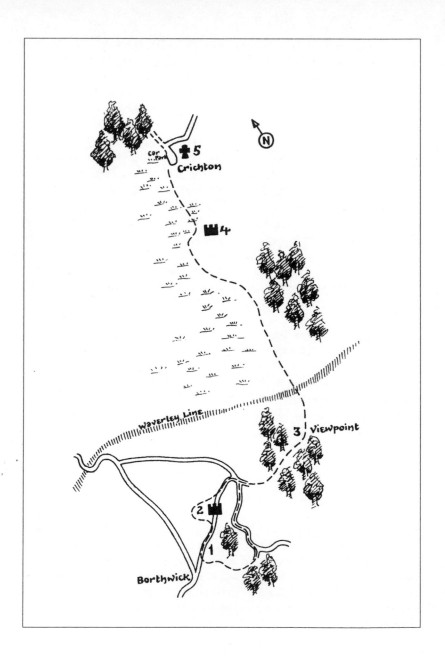

Walk down to the road to the left and round the front of
Currie House. Follow the path up through the woods to the
viewpoint (3).

From this vantage point, the whole of the valley comes into view. The valley was formed by glacial action during the last ice age, and was widened by the meltwater from the ice which was channeled through the valley to the sea. The route of **the Waverley Line**, the old Edinburgh to Carlisle railway, can be seen from the viewpoint.

Continue along the footpath and cross over the Waverley Line.
Walk on past the mature deciduous woods to the right is
Crichton Castle.

Crichton Castle (4), standing high above the River Tyne, is one of the most dramatic ruins in Midlothian. Originally built by John de Crichton in the 14th century as a fortified tower, it was later extended by his son, William, whose association with **James I** led to a marked improvement in the family's fortunes. At one point, William was the keeper of Edinburgh Castle, and despite a temporary setback in his fortunes, he retained his position as an important nobleman. During his long career, William Crichton was involved in the murders of at least two members of **the Black Douglas** family. Perhaps as a result of this he found it necessary to establish a church at Crichton to expunge his guilt. The Crichton's tenure of the castle came to an abrupt end in the time of William's grandson when involvement in yet another conspiracy led to the confiscation of all the family's lands and possessions at the end of the 15th century.

James III gave the lands of Crichton to one of his favourites, Lord Bothwell. Unfortunately for the new Lord of Crichton, the king was murdered, after falling from his horse at the Battle of Sauchieburn in 1488, by rebels allegedly led by his eldest son, who then became James IV, and Bothwell was forced into permanent exile. Following in the footsteps of his late father James IV then gave Crichton and the Bothwell title to one of his favourites, Sir Patrick Hepburn, Lord of Hailes.

It remained in the family until the 17th century inhabited by one or two curious individuals. The most famous of these was James Hepburn, 4th Earl of Bothwell, who was the third husband of **Mary Queen of Scots**. Mary herself visited Crichton Castle in 1562 for the marriage of her half brother to Bothwell's sister. **James Hepburn** was a sinister character

who was implicated in the murder of the Queen's sec- ond husband Lord Darnley in Febru- ary 1567. Having aroused the jeal- ousy of the nobil- ity, Bothwell was accused of treason and forced to flee the country. He was eventually cor- nered in Norway after a career of piracy and was imprisoned, tor- tured and driven insane. After eleven years in a variety of prisons, he died at **Dragsholm Castle** in Denmark in 1578. An interesting postscript to this was the fact that his mummified body remained on display as a macabre tourist attraction at a church near Dragsholm until 1977.

After the flight of the fourth Earl, the castle passed to the hands of one of his relatives, Francis Stewart, in 1581. A cosmopolitan and well travelled individual, he introduced the Italian Renaissance influences that can still be seen at Crichton today. However, like many of his predecessors, he was an unpredictable character who, having at one time enjoyed the confidence of the king - he was Lord High Admiral of Scotland - ended his days in exile. He was the last Lord of Crichton, and by the 1650's the castle was falling into ruin.

Sir Walter Scott's interest in the antiquities of Scotland led him to lament the pitiful state of many of Scotland's castles, and his inclusion of Crichton in the poem *Marmion* may well have saved it from total obliteration. The oft quoted couplet from *Marmion*,

> "O what a tangled web we weave,
> When first we practise to deceive!"

accurately sums up the atmosphere of intrigue that surrounded the Lords of Crichton.

Entering the castle through the door beside the massive 14th century tower, you come to the courtyard. On the right is the most unexpected feature of the castle, the extraordinary **Italian Renaissance style facade** built by the fifth Earl in the late 16th century. With its diamond faceted design and colonnaded walkway underneath, this part of the building clearly derives from the architecture of southern Italy and from the fifth Earl's travels in that region. It is unique in Scotland, but similar examples are still to be seen in the southern mediterranean.

In the grounds of the castle stands a large **stable block** with an interesting horseshoe shaped window above the entrance.

Beyond Crichton Castle is Crichton Church.

Crichton Church (5) was built in the 16th century by William Crichton. Now a fairly unremarkable building, it has been much altered over the years.

> *Return to Borthwick either by the same route or along the roads. To return by road, walk up past the church to the first junction and turn left. After about a mile and a half, turn left and follow the road back to Borthwick.*

9
Bonaly Country Park Hill Walks

Bonaly Tower
Countryside Walks
Capelaw Hill

Opening times
Bonaly Tower not open to the public
Country Park open all year

Recommended Maps
Bartholomew Pentland Hills

Directions to start
From Lothian Road, continue up to Bruntsfield and
turn right off Morningside Road into Colinton Road.
Continue to the end of Colinton Road and take the
left fork at the traffic lights into Woodhall Road. Then
take the third road on the left, Bonaly Road, and
continue up past Bonaly Tower to the car park.

Starting Point
the car park (1)

OS Map Ref 212675

Bonaly Tower was owned by **Lord Cockburn** who was responsible for developing it from a simple farmhouse to the grand, rambling Scots Baronial country house it is today. He was so taken with the house that he was moved to say "unless some avenging angel shall expel me, I shall never leave this paradise."

These Pentland walks were amongst his favourites, and it was here that Lord Cockburn first had the idea of starting a new, classical school in the city, which was to be **Edinburgh Academy**. It was said that the city Fathers objected to a new school being built to rival their own, and commissioned St Stephens Church to be built directly in front of the school in the New Town to overshadow it. But the school was a tremendous success, counting amongst its pupils **James Clerk Maxwell**, later to write the seminal work *A Treatise on Electricity and Magnetism* which established him in the scientific world alongside Newton and Einstein.

These walks in the Bonaly Country Park are of varying lengths and difficuty. (i) and (ii) are easy walks and can be tackled by anyone, but (iii) is substantially longer.

(i) Torduff and Clubbiedean Reservoirs
Distance 2 miles

Walk up from the car park and into the park. Turn right
where the paths diverge and the walk along to the reservoirs
is fairly gentle.

(ii) Bonaly Reservoir
Distance 2 miles

Walk up from the car park, into the park, and continue
straight up the path between Capelaw Hill and Harbour Hill.
From Bonaly Reservoir there are easy climbs to either of the
hills.

(iii) The Circular Walk

Distance 5 miles

Walk up to Bonaly Reservoir as in (ii), and then continue walking between Capelaw Hill and Harbour Hill. Where the paths meet at the ruined cottage, turn right and walk through the Maiden's Cleuch between Harbour Hill and Bell's Hill. At the gate, take the path to the right and walk down past the car park to the road. Turn right and then right again at East Kinleith. This takes you round Clubbiedean and Torduff Reservoirs and back to the start.

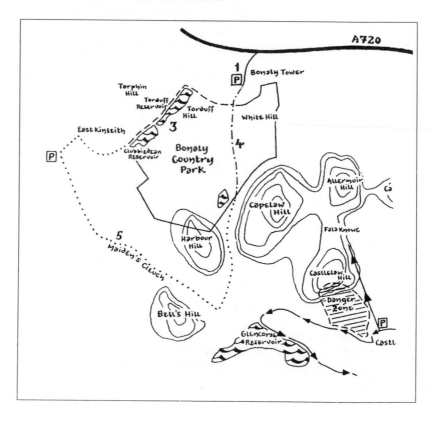

10
Fala Moor to Soutra Aisle

Fala Village
Moor Walk
Tower Remains
Soutra Aisle

Recommended Map
Ordnance Survey Landranger 66

Distance 5 miles

Directions to Start
South east from Edinburgh on the A68, through
Dalkeith and Pathhead to Fala.

Starting point
Fala Village (1)

OS Map Ref 438610

Fala Village has a delightful kirk with views over to the Lammermuir Hills.

From the village, walk up to the main road at turn left. On the
right is a rough track which leads up onto the moor itself.
Walk through the wooded section and through the gate onto
the moor.

On the right after about a mile is the ruined tower which looks more substantial from a distance than it really is. All that is left of **Fala Luggie (2)**, a 16th century house which provided accomodation for travellers, is a single wall. Although it seems unlikely in the late 20th century, this was an important route from Scotland to England and the owners of Fala Luggie would have made a good living from the passing trade.

Many armies have passed through Fala Moor, and it was here that **James I** led his army in 1542 to counter an English invasion. On their arrival at Fala Moor, the Scots found that the Auld Enemy had retreated back over the border, and James thought this would be an excellent opportunity to attack. His troops, however, did not agree and refused to continue, believing that the action was solely for the benefit of France. A humiliated James was forced to abandon the invasion.

Today the main activity on the moor is sheep farming and peat extraction.

Before the trees, where the track goes on to Brothershiels,
there is a path to the left which goes over the Brothershiels
Burn and straight up to Upper Brotherstone Cottage. Take this
path and follow it onto the track to the left of the cottage and
down to Gilston.

At the main road, turn left and walk up the road for about a
mile. On the right is Soutra Aisle.

Soutra Aisle (3) was a mediaeval hospice run by the Augustinian order. It was frequented by travellers journeying between Scotland and England along **Dere Street**, the nearby Roman road. It was also regarded as neutral ground for the treatment of battle wounds. All that remains today

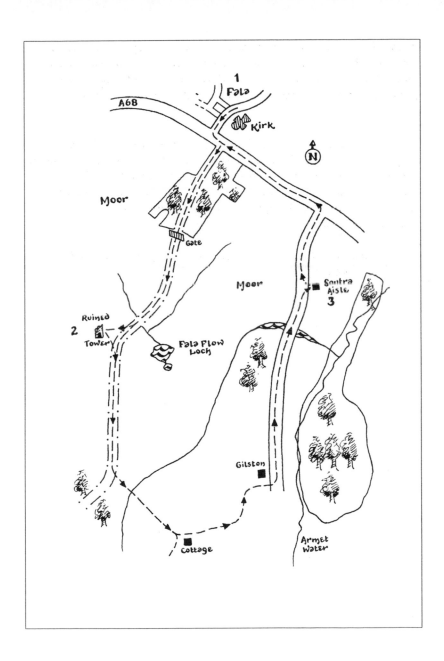

is a single stone building and a complex of archaeological remains. Excavations have been going on for several years, and only a small fraction of the original site has so far been unearthed. The hospice and its outbuildings may well have spread across the nearby fields, a theory supported by recent test borings.

The present excavation is on the site of a **bakehouse and cesspit**, and fragments of mediaeval stained glass have been found. A more significant discovery can be seen in a pit at the centre of the excavations. The evidence suggests that an army used this building as a latrine during a short stay here, and the layer of material they left has yielded interesting information on the diet of mediaeval people.

> *Continue walking until you reach the A68 again, and turn left and follow the road back to Fala.*

The Pentlands

Bavelaw

Swanston

Whitekirk

Tithe Barn

Preston Mill

Dirleton

Borthwick

Whitekirk

Morham

Dalmeny

Morham

St Mary's

Haddington

Whitekirk

Whitekirk

11
Nine Mile Burn and the Kips

West Kip
East Kip
Scald Law

Recommended Map
Bartholomew Pentland Hills

Distance 4 miles

Habbie's Howe Country Hotel (est 1643)
tea, coffee, beer garden

Directions to start
A702 south from Edinburgh to Nine Mile Burn. Turn right at the petrol station for the village.

Starting Point
Nine Mile Burn, at the gate on the corner (1).

OS Map Ref 178578

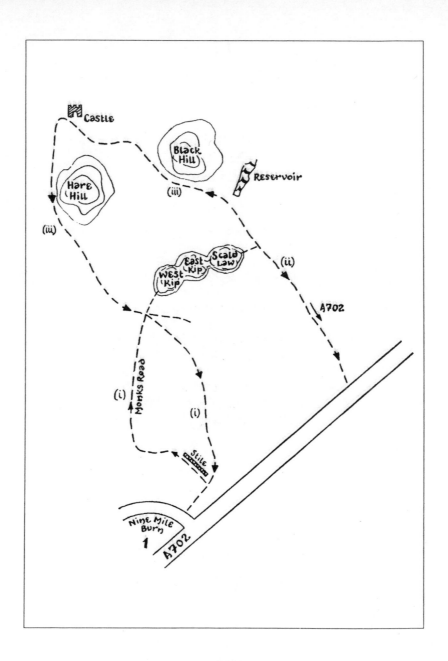

Castle

Black Hill

Hare Hill

Reservoir

(iii)

(iii)

Scald Law

East Kip

West Kip

(ii)

A702

Monks Road

(i)

(i)

Stile

Nine Mile Burn

1

A702

The first section of this walk follows the route of the old Roman road, as does the road through the village heading towards Carlops.

*Go through the gate and walk up to the first dry stone wall. Turn left just before the wall and walk up to the stile at the top of the field. Once over the stile, turn left and follow the path up the **Monks Road** which runs parallel to the Monks Burn. At the 1500 ft post the path ahead provides access to the top of **West Kip (1806 ft)**, **East Kip (1737 ft)** and **Scald Law (1899 ft)**.*

From here there are three alternatives.

(i) The quickest way back to the starting point is to return to the 1500 ft post and take the path to the left of the Monks Road which leads to Nine Mile Burn. **Distance 4 miles.**

(ii) If you continue over Scald Law and down to the right at the next path, the descent to the A702 and return to Nine Mile Burn along the road is far less demanding. **Distance 5 miles.**

(iii) To extend the walk considerably, turn left after the descent from Scald Law and walk along the Kirk Road to the south west end of Loganlee Reservoir. Turn left and walk past the Logan Burn waterfall and between the Black Hill and Hare Hill to Bavelaw Castle, round the far side of Hare Hill and back up to the 1500 ft post at the top of the Monks Road. **Distance 8 miles.**

12
Nine Mile Burn to Carlops

(i) by North Esk Reservoir - 3 miles
(ii) by North Esk Reservoir,
Borestane and Bavelaw Castle - 12 miles
(iii) by North Esk Reservoir, Borestane, Harperrig,
Cauldstane Slap and Baddinsgill - 17 miles

Recommended Map
Bartholomew Pentland Hills

Habbie's Howe Country Hotel (est 1643)
Nine Mile Burn
tea, coffee, beer garden
Allan Ramsay Hotel
Carlops
bar meals, restaurant

Directions to Start
A702 south from Edinburgh to Nine Mile Burn.
Turn right at the petrol station for the village.

Starting Point
Habbie's Howe Hotel (1).

OS Map Ref 178578

(i) Distance 3 miles

Walk past the Habbie's Howe Hotel and towards Carlops along the route of the old Roman road. At Spittal, follow the path to the right (to Balerno by Borestane). Walk for about a mile through the gap between Spittal Hill and Paties Hill and on to the North Esk Reservoir. Walk past the cottage to the post and turn left towards Carlops. At Fairliehope there is a choice of paths to Carlops. Take the path to the right and walk down to the village. Carlops, with its massive rock, was originally a weaving town, and the hotel at one end is appropriately named after Allan Ramsay the poet, who was, according to Sir Walter Scott, well known for his drinking.

To return to Nine Mile Burn, walk through the village and across the River North Esk and along the path a little further on to the left.

(ii) Distance 12 miles

Follow the same route as (i) to the North Esk Reservoir and turn right. Continue up past the reservoir and onto Borestane, some curious rocks of indeterminate origin which mark the northern boundary of Peeblesshire. Keep walking up the path, over the Bavelaw Burn, and turn right opposite the entrance to Listonshiels. Follow the Old Road on past West Rigg and East Rigg and turn right at Marchbank, past the Red Moss Wildlife Reserve and up the tree lined avenue towards Bavelaw Castle. Instead of turning left to the castle, turn right and walk up round Hare Hill. Continue on to the 1500 ft post in the shadow of West Kip and turn right down the Monks Road to Nine Mile Burn.

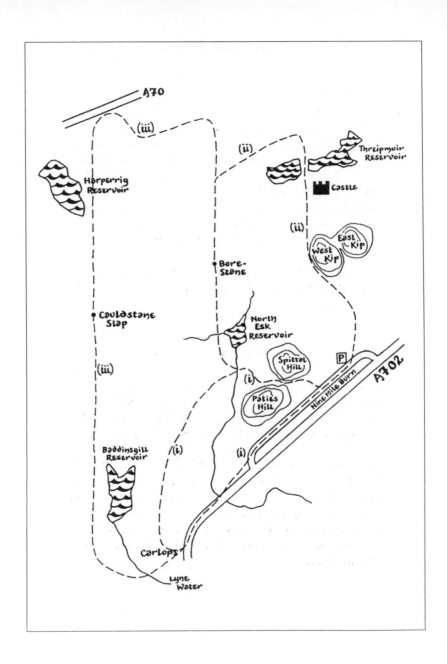

(iii) Distance 17 miles

Follow the same route as (ii) as far as Listonshiels, but instead
of turning right, carry straight on. At the end of the straight
tree lined road turn left and walk up towards Buteland Hill,
keeping Temple House and Buteland House on the right. Past
Buteland House, turn right and cross the Water of Leith. Once
over the river, turn right and then left onto the A70. About a
mile down the A70 is a turning to the left at the Old Toll
House which will take you straight up past Harperrig Reservoir, on to Cauldstane Slap at 1430 ft and down past Baddinsgill reservoir. This is an old Drove Road, and the name
Cauldstane simply describes this high, bleak, stoney pass. At
the end of the reservoir walk over the Baddinsgill Burn, past
the farm buildings, over the Glen Ely burn and then turn left at
the post. Cross over the Lyne Water and walk down the path
which runs parallel to the river. At the next junction, take the
path to the left and the old road will take you back to Carlops.
The return from Carlops to Nine Mile Burn is described in
section (i).

13
Haddington

William the Lion's Royal Palace
William Adam Town House
Jane Welsh Carlyle Museum
Nungate Bridge
St Marys Church
Haddington House and Garden

Opening Times
Jane Welsh Carlyle museum open April-Sept,
Wed-Sat 2-5pm
St Marys Church - 10am-4pm Mon-Sat,
1-4pm Sunday, April-Sept
Haddington House Garden open daily, admission free

Cafes/Teashops
The Carlyle, High Street
St Mary's Church, Sidegate

Directions to start
Follow the A1 east from Edinburgh to Haddington.
The Adam Town House with its tall spire stands at the
end of Court Street and dominates the centre of
town. Continue past this landmark and down to the
end of High Street. Turn right and continue down
Sidegate to St Mary's Church on the left.

Starting Point: St Mary's Church (1)
OS Map Reference 514739

St Mary's Collegiate Church dates from the 14th century and was built on the site of a 13th century Franciscan Friary. This earlier building included the Lamp of Lothian Chapel destroyed by Edward III in 1355. The church bears a striking similarity to St Giles Cathedral in Edinburgh, although it is longer than St Giles and lacks the distinctive crown tower. Until the Reformation, St Mary's came under the control of the Bishop of St Andrews, and it was here that **George Wishart**, friend and mentor of John Knox, preached his last sermon before being burned at the stake for heresy in St Andrews in 1546. Haddington was besieged by Henry VIII's army from 1547 to 1549 and St Mary's was virtually destroyed. It was not until 1560 that some of the damage done to St Mary's was repaired by **John Knox**, and for four hundred years only the nave was in use.

The daunting task of **restoration** began in 1971 and was completed in 1973. Employing such innovatory techniques as fibreglass vaulting, the results are remarkably authentic. An exhibition in the church tells the complete story of this unique and massive undertaking.

On a sunny day, one of the most unusual features of St Mary's is the effect of the light streaming in through the contemporary **stained glass** of the south transept, casting a mosaic of light over the elaborate Seton family memorial of 1682. The Choir contains a number of interesting tombs, and above the communion table at the east end there is a carving depicting the Haddington goat, which was discovered when the foundations were being excavated. At the east end (on the south side) the ravages of time can be clearly seen in the uneven pillars and undulating masonry.

As you leave by the west door, you pass through the excellent and reasonably priced **teashop**. There is also a **gift shop and brass rubbing** facilities are available every Monday, Thursday, Friday and Saturday during the summer from 1-4pm.

> *Leave the church and turn right. Walk through the churchyard and through the gate into the garden of the adjacent Haddington House.*

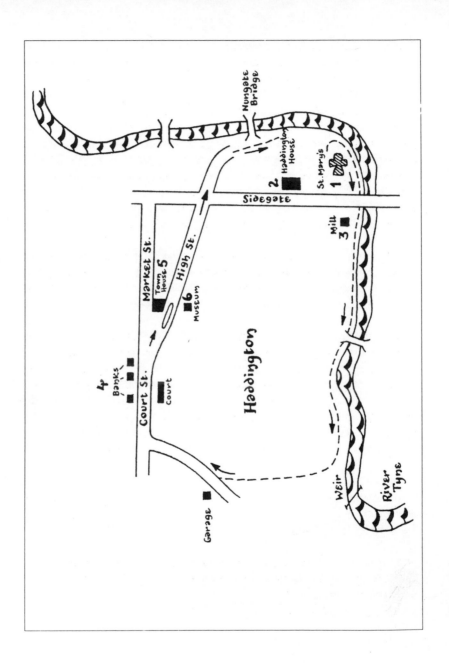

Nungate Bridge

Haddington House

St. Mary's

2

1

Sidegate

Mill

3

Market St.

High St.

Town House

5

6

Museum

Court St.

Banks

4

Court

Garage

Haddington

Weir

River Tyne

St. Mary's Haddington.

Haddington House (2) is owned by the Lamp of Lothian Collegiate Trust and its garden, which is open to the public all the year round, is a representation of a garden of the old Scots style. Entering the garden you will see the Mount on your right, an unusual vantage point, and on your left a Boxed Hornbeam walk and a Laburnum Alley. The garden also contains an apple tree planted by the Queen in 1973, a mulberry planted by the Queen Mother in 1976 as well as a comprehensive selection of fruit trees - fig, damson, pear, apricot and plum. There is also a small sunken garden close to the house. Opposite the entrance to the gardens is **Summerfield**, an 18th century mansion house with a pair of unusual pedimented pavillions by the roadside. These were formerly used as a stable and coach house.

> *Walk back through the gate into the churchyard, turn left, and walk out through the gates onto the riverside walkway.*

On your left is the 16th century **Nungate Bridge**, notable for its uneven western arch, and at this side of the bridge is **Lady Kitty's doocot**.

> *Walk past St Mary's church and continue along to the Mill.*

Poldrate Mill (3), also known as the old Kirk Mill, is the most recent of a series of mills to have occupied this site since the 13th century.

Carry on, keeping the mill to your right, until you reach the weir. Cross the small bridge over the mill lade and walk up to the garage. Turn right past Knox court and at the end of Knox place turn right into Court Street at the Railway Hotel.

Opposite the Railway. Hotel is a statue of **Robert Ferguson of Raith MP**, Lord Lieutenant of Fife, "a kind landlord, a liberal dispenser of wealth."

Haddington has been a Royal Burgh since the time of **David I** in the 12th century, although much of the town centre was built in the 18th century and retains the classical character of that time. As you walk down Court Street and past the quaint 19th century Police station on your right the impressive **classical townhouses (4)**, now mostly occupied by banks, can be seen on the left. A little further down on the right are the Court buildings, built on the site of the **12th century Royal Palace** of King William I of Scotland - William the Lion. In front of the Court Building is

Town House, Haddington.

the monument to George, 8th Earl of Tweedale and Lord Lieutenant of Haddingtonshire (1787-1876), Field Marshal and one-time governor of Madras. A little further on is the grotesque Samson fountain which stands opposite the neo-classical Wm Low supermarket. Dominating Court Street is the **William Adam Town House (5).**

Walk past the right hand side of the Town House, and down a close on the right is the house where **Jane Welsh Carlyle lived (6),** *now a small museum of Carlyle memorabilia. By far the most interesting exhibit is a poster from the Napoleonic Wars.*

The Consequences of Bonaparte's
Succeeding in his Designs

Univerfal Pillage.
Men of all Parties Slaughtered.
Women of all Ranks Violated.
Children Murdered.
Trade Ruined.
The Labouring Claffes thrown out of
employment.
Famine with all its Horrors.
Defpotifm Triumphant.
The remaining Inhabitants carried away by
Ship–Loads to Foreign Lands.

Sixpence per Dozen.

On leaving the delightful **museum garden** turn right, and on the left after 50yds is the house where **Samuel Smiles** (1812-1904), the influential Victorian author of *Self Help*, was born. He is remembered today as the promoter of the 'gospel of work', and the right wing 'Victorian values' he cherished still find support today. As well as *Self-Help* (1859), he wrote *Character* (1871), *Thrift* (1875), and *Duty* (1880).

"A place for everything and everything in its place"
From *Thrift* by **Samuel Smiles**

A little further on is the **Market Cross** with the symbolic Haddington goat on top.

> *Walk to the end of High Street and on the corner with Sidegate is a plaque marking the level the river reached during the flood of October 1775. Continue down Church Street, opposite the plaque, past the Nungate Bridge and back to St Mary's.*

14
South from Haddington

St Mary's Church
Lennoxlove
Robert Burns
Morham
John Knox

Opening Times
Lennoxlove open Easter weekend and May-Sept,
Wed, Sat and Sun, 2-5pm

Recommended Map
Ordnance Survey Landranger 66

Walking Distance 11 miles

Tearooms
St Mary's Church
Lennoxlove

Directions to Start
A1 east from Edinburgh to Haddington. Once in the
town centre, go down past the Adam Town House
and down High Street. At the end of High Street turn
right into Sidegate and St Mary's is on the left.

Starting Point St Mary's Church (1)
OS Map Ref 519736

Walk through the graveyard of St Mary's Church, details of which are given in Walk 13, and out through the gate onto the riverside walk. Turn right onto the path and walk down to the Poldrate Mill. Follow the path along the side of the River Tyne. Cross the bridge over the river and walk up to the stile. Turn left over the stile and walk back up to the road.

Back at the road, turn right and continue along beside the A6137 heading south. About a third of a mile further on is the road to the left up to Lennoxlove which goes past Lennoxlove Mains farm.

Lennoxlove (2), originally known as Lethington, developed from a massive fortified tower into the impressive country mansion that is now the seat of **the Duke of Hamilton.** For three hundred years it belonged to the Maitlands, an influential Scots family, (one member of the family died at the Battle of Flodden in 1513 and another, while Secretary of State to Mary Queen of Scots, was involved in the plot to murder Darnley) until it was bought by the trustees of the Duchess of Lennox in 1703.

The unusual name was chosen by Frances Teresa Stewart, known as **La Belle Stewart**, who turned down Charles II in favour of Charles Stewart, Duke of Richmond and Lennox. He died young, falling overboard during a party on a ship while Ambassador to Denmark, and his wife left instructions that after her death (in 1702) a house should be bought for her cousin, the Master of Blantyre, and named in memory of her husband - thus Lethington became Lennoxlove. The house remained in the family until it was bought by the Duke of Hamilton in 1946. The Hamiltons had been forced to abandon Hamilton Palace after the mine workings which had made their fortune forced the demolition of their 16th century family seat.

Most of the contents of the house were brought from **Hamilton Palace** and reflect the history of the present owners. Of particular interest are some of the portraits that line the staircase. Beside the strange Victorian hands and feet is a portrait of **the 4th Duke of Hamilton** who was killed in one of the most celebrated duels of the 18th century. He became involved in a long running dispute with **Lord Mohun** - an unsavoury

Sundial at Lennoxlove.

character who had been accused of murder on three previous occasions and whose father was killed in a duel - which culminated in an exceptionally savage duel fought in Hyde Park in 1712. The seconds of both sides apparently joined in, Hamilton killed Mohun, but was then unsportingly stabbed in the back and killed by one of Mohun's seconds.

Another portrait depicts the 8th Duke as a young man on the Grand Tour. It is particularly notable for the presence of his tutor Dr Moore and his 15 year old son John. Later to become a national hero in the Peninsular War, **General Sir John Moore** died during the retreat from Corunna in 1809.

At the end of the landing is a small elegant table which belonged to **Napoleon** and bears his silver crest. In the bedroom to the right is a fabulously ornate ebony bed inlaid with ivory which is of Indo-Portuguese origin. It was given to the 10th Duke by Napoleon's sister. The significance of this unusually splendid gift can only be guessed at.

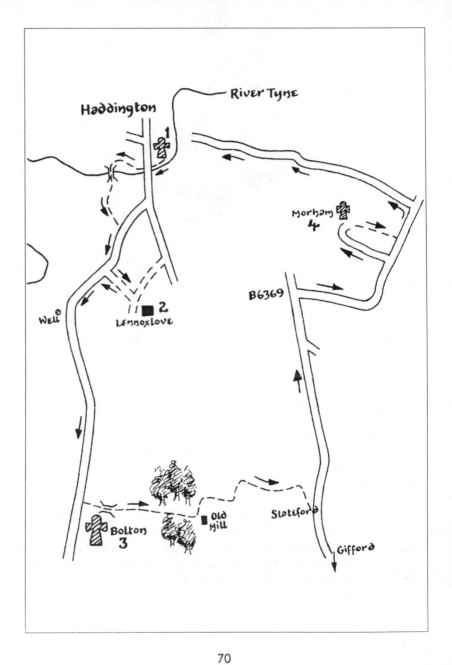

Haddington

River Tyne

1

Morham
4

Well

Lennoxlove
2

B6369

Bolton
3

Old
Mill

Slateford

Gifford

Moving through the beautifully proportioned Blue and Yellow Rooms, the most striking feature is the **tortoishell cabinet** given to La Belle Stewart by Charles II. Ornamented with a crown and hearts, it signified the king's continuing admiration for her after the death of her husband.

Also at Lennoxlove are the death masks of **Mary Queen of Scots** and of **Sir Walter Scott**, the latter having a remarkably tall forehead. Beside the death mask of Mary Queen of Scots is the ornate silver casket that contained the **'Casket Letters'** which, although probably forged by her enemies, implicated the Queen in the murder of her husband Lord Darnley. In the same room are two hagbuts and a collection of swords.

The next room visited, and perhaps the most impressive at Lennoxlove, is **the Great Hall**. Situated in the oldest part of the building, the 14th century tower, much of what can be seen here - such as the large windows - dates from the 17th century. Further alterations were made this century including the addition of the elaborate fireplace with its carvings of a monkey, a caveman and a lion.

Downstairs is the Undercroft where you can see the **well** and the **pit prison**. In the ante room there is a collection of memorabilia, mostly relating to the 14th and 15th Dukes, such as **Rudolph Hess's map and compass**, various aviation paintings - the 14th Duke was the first man to fly over Everest (1933) - and mementos of the 15th Duke's exploits as a motor racing driver.

On leaving the house, it is worth visiting the garden with its unusual sundial and 'Politicians Walk'.

> *Walk back to the A6137 and turn left. On the right through the lay-by is the well and the nearby monument with the inscription*

"Near this spot stood the house in which lived and died the mother brother and sister of Scotland's National Poet, **Robert Burns**."

> *Continue down the road to Bolton and to the right of the* **village kirk (3)** *is the Burns family grave.*

Burn's mother Agnes, of whom his sister wrote "(she had) dark eyes often ablaze with a temper difficult of control", died in 1820 at the age of 88. His brother Gilbert who died in 1827 aged 67 and various other members of the family also lie here.

> "I have a younger brother who supports my aged mother, another still younger brother, and three sisters in a farm. On my last return from Edinburgh, it cost me about £180 to save them from ruin...and I thought that throwing a little filial piety and fraternal affection in the scale in my favour might help to smooth matters at the 'grand reckoning'."
> **Robert Burns 1789**

From the church gate, retrace your steps a few yards to the old forge building with its characteristically wide chimney and walk down the road to the right. At the bottom of the hill, cross the bridge and walk up the farm track keeping the stream on your left. Carry straight on, over the gate, and just before the woods the path forks. Ignore the left fork and carry on through the avenue of trees to the end of the wood. Carry on over the stile to the Coulston Old Mill. Turn left on the track and then right and right again and follow the track along to the main road, the B6369, at Slateford.

Turn left and walk about a mile to the second road on the right. This leads to Morham. After about a mile you will pass Morham Loanhead, and a little further on a small road on the left leads to **Morham Church (4).**

There has been a church on this site since the 8th century, but the present church dates from 1724. Although this is the smallest parish in East Lothian, over the years it has produced a disproportionate number of interesting characters.

Sir Herbert de Morham, a distinguished soldier, was captured at the Battle of Dunbar in 1296. After being held prisoner by the English for some time, he was released only on condition that he should serve **Edward I,**

the *Hammer of the Scots*. Sir Herbert, however, supported a later Scots rising and was again taken prisoner by the English. Edward I took no chances this time and released everyone except Sir Herbert who was executed after rotting in prison for six years. **Mary Queen of Scots** third husband, **Bothwell,** was staying at Morham when he became involved in the plot to kill her second husband, **Lord Darnley;** Queen Anne's advocate, Sir David Dalrymple whose family owned much of the parish, gained notoriety for his involvement in the massacre of Glencoe; and in the 17th century, Morham was the focus of a famous murder inquiry in which the chief prosecutor was **Sir George 'Bluidy' MacKenzie**, persecutor of the Covenanters.

Philip Stansfield was accused and convicted of the murder of his father after a suspiciously quick burial raised doubts about the manner of his death. The body was disinterred and placed in the church where the traditional ritual of the accused person touching the body of the deceased was carried out. If the body bled, the accused was guilty. Unfortunately for Stansfield, it did, and his conviction and execution followed swiftly. He was hung, drawn and quartered and his head was placed on the east gate of Haddington.

The churchyard contains some of the gravestones of the family of **John Knox**. Near the church door is a stone marking the grave of William Knox, grand-nephew of John Knox, who died in 1660. John Knox was himself born in the parish, at Mainshill Farm.

A few yards from the church are the gravestones of Mrs De Pree and other members of the De Pree family. They had been living nearby at Beech Hill House since the First World War, when a bizarre tragedy struck in October 1944. A British plane crashed onto the house killing everyone inside, except for Colonel De Pree. The house has since been rebuilt.

On leaving the churchyard, turn left and follow the right of way which runs alongside the burn back to the main road. Turn left and left again at the next junction, turn left and follow the road back to Haddington.

15
Athelstaneford to East Fortune

Hopetoun Monument
Garleton Castle
Athelstaneford Church
The Scottish Flag
Doocot
Barnes Castle
East Fortune Museum of Flight
Motor Museum

Opening Times
East Fortune Air Museum open 7 days a week
10.30am-4.30pm between Easter and the end of
September. Admission free.
Motor Museum open daily at 10am, admission £1.80

Recommended Map
Ordnance Survey Landranger 66

Distance 4 miles

Tearoom
East Fortune Airfield

Directions to Start
A1 east from Edinburgh to Haddington. Left onto the
A6137 then right onto the B1343 to Athelstaneford.

Starting Point Athelstaneford Church (1)
OS Map Reference 534773

On the way to the starting point you will pass **the Hopetoun Monument**, and the car park is on the right just after the turn onto the B1343. The monument was erected on Byres Hill, a volcanic plug, to the memory of John Hope 4th Earl of Hopetoun (1765-1823) by his tenants. Gifted to the District Council by Sir James and Lady Miller in 1977, the most interesting thing about the monument is the view from the top.

A little further on, on the right just past the road junction, is **Garleton Castle** a ruin dating from the 16th century. Many of these old fortifications are now used as storage space for nearby farms, and another example of this is Barnes castle a little further on.

Athelstaneford Church's main claim to fame is **the Scottish flag**, which always flies in the grounds. Tradition has it that an army of Scots and Pictish warriors gathered near here in order to defeat an advancing Northumbrian army led by **Athelstan**. Athelstan was killed in the ensuing battle close to the spot where Athelstaneford Mains Farm now stands, half a mile south east of the church. Before the battle had started, the blue sky was criss-crossed with clouds in the shape of **the Cross of St Andrew**. This proved to be a lucky omen and after the victory the Scots made a blue and white flag to commemorate the event, and thus the Cross of St Andrew was adopted as the national emblem. This historic event is commemorated by a memorial in the churchyard, unveiled in November 1965.

The original church was built on this site in 1176 by the mother of **William the Lion**, but the present church dates from the end of the 18th century and was much altered at the end of the 19th century.

Inside the church is a memorial to **Sir David Kinloch of Gilmerton**, who was responsible for many of the buildings in the village which were built in the 1780's as part of a model village. The pan-tiled vernacular cottages, little changed since the 18th century, are some of the best in East Lothian. Also remembered in the church is **John Home** (1722-1808), minister here from 1745-57, who resigned from his post to concentrate on playwriting following the success of the tragedy *Douglas*. *Douglas* was not his first attempt at writing for the stage, and Home had been bitterly disappointed when *Agis* was turned down by Garrick, the theatre impresario, ten years

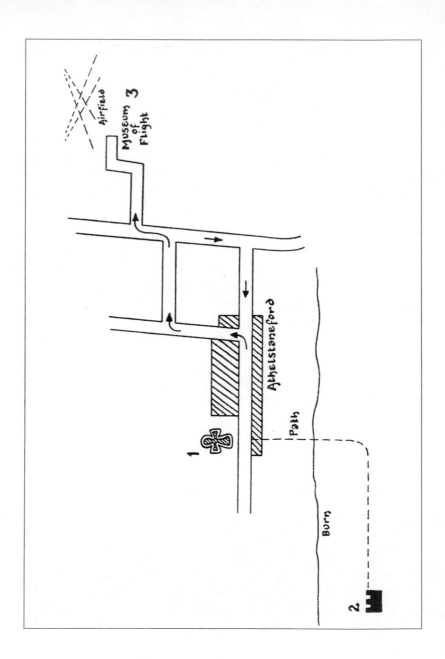

Airfield

Museum
of
Flight 3

Athelstaneford

Path

1

Burn

2

earlier. At that time, Home had gone to Shakespeare's monument at Westminster Abbey and written:

"Image of Shakespeare! to this place I come
To ease my bursting bosom at thy tomb;
For neither Greek nor Roman poet fired
My fancy first, thee chiefly I admired;
And day and night revolving still my page
I hoped, like thee, to shake the British stage;
But cold neglect is now my only mead
And heavy falls it on so proud a head."

Home recovered from this bitter experience, and when *Douglas* opened in Edinburgh at the end of 1756 it caused a tremendous stir. When it opened in London just four months later, Home's fame was assured. Garrick, now regretting having turned down Douglas, asked Home if he could stage *Agis*. Unfortunately his original judgement had been right, and *Agis* flopped disasterously. Home was never again to repeat the success of *Douglas*, and, after five more failures, gave up.

The churchyard contains a number of interesting tombs and gravestones dating from the 17th to the 20th century. To the left of the gate is a memorial dedicated by Colonel Hunt and the officers of RAF station East Fortune to the memory of Lieutenant Lynn Newton Bissell, aged 21, and Lieutenant Eric Wensley Bragg, age 22, "who died in the service of their country at East Fortune 31 October 1918."

Just outside the back wall of the churchyard is a typical 16th century doocot in an excellent state of preservation. From here there are also views over to North Berwick Law.

Opposite the church there is a path which is slightly overgrown but leads up towards **Barnes Castle (2)** *which is now part of Barney Mains Farm. Where the path forks, take the path* *to the left, go over the stile, across the burn and follow the fence up to the ridge. Barnes Castle, visible from a little further along to the right, was built by the Seton family in the 16th century but never completed. Judging by what remains today, it would have been very extensive.*

The walk from the village to **the East Fortune Museum of Flight (3)** *is about a mile. Walk along to the middle of the village and turn left with the B1343. Take the next turning on the right and walk up to the B1347. Turn left here and the entrance to the airfield is on the right.*

East Fortune is a former RAF station which was operational in both world wars, and it was from here that the airship **R34** began its historic Atlantic crossing in the summer of 1919. The museum now houses a wide ranging collection of aircraft and aeronautical memorabilia. Of particular interest are: the **Supermarine Spitfire, Comet** airliner, **Vulcan** bomber, nuclear missile, **ME163 rocket plane, Lightning** jet fighter and a combustion chamber from a **V2 rocket.**

The **Vulcan bomber,** XM 597, was brought out of retirement in 1982 to take part in the not entirely successful bombing raids on the Falkland Islands. It made headlines when mid air re-fuelling difficulties on the way back to Ascension Island forced it to land in Rio.

The **V2** combustion chamber is from the type of rocket the Germans used against London in the later stages of the Second World War. V2's rose to 60 miles, reached a speed of 3,600 miles per hour and carried a ton of explosives.

The tiny **Messerschmitt 163**, or Komet as it was known, was introduced in 1944 to combat the US Airforce's daylight raids on Germany. Powered by a rocket motor, it used an extremely volatile fuel mixture which gave it tremendous speed but only 5-8 minutes in the air. It dropped its wheels on take-off and landing it on its ski often proved fatal.

Me 163 'KOMET'.

To return to Athelstaneford, turn left out of the gate and take the second road on the right.

On your return journey to Edinburgh, if you are interested in classic cars and motoring memorabilia, you may like to take a diversion to the **Myreton Motor Museum (OS Ref 487794)**. Housed in what appears to be a quaint antique garage just off the A6137, vehicles on display include a 1954 Cooper racing car, a World War Two Daimler Scout Car, and a Wolseley owned by the same person from 1937-1972 and never driven in the rain.

16
Hailes Castle to Preston Mill

Hailes Castle
River Tyne Walk
East Linton
Preston Mill
Phantassie Doocot

Opening Times
Hailes Castle open summer Mon-Sat 9.30-7pm, Sun 2-7; winter key available from keeper
Preston Mill open 24 March to 30 Sept, Mon-Sat 10-1 & 2-5, Sun 2-5pm. October Mon-Sat 10-1 & 2-4.30pm, Sun 2-4.30pm. November Sat 10-12.30 & 2-4.30pm, Sun 2-4.30pm

Recommended Map
Ordnance Survey Landranger 67

Walking Distance 5 miles

Directions to Start
A1 east from Edinburgh, past Haddington and right at the signpost for Hailes Castle.

Starting Point Hailes Castle (1)
OS Map Reference 574758

Hailes Castle was built on a rocky promontory overlooking the River Tyne in the 13th century. By the 16th century it was an important stronghold owned by the **Earl of Bothwell.** In 1548 Henry VIII's invading army captured Hailes during the 'Rough Wooing'. The Earl of Arran re-took the castle and ownership reverted to the Bothwell family in 1556. **Mary Queen of Scots** stayed here in 1557 on her way to Dunbar. Like so many other Scots castles, its ruinous state is entirely due to the actions of Cromwell's army in 1650.

What remains of the castle is a mixture of 13th, 14th and 15th century building. It is unusual in that, unlike many Scots castles of the period there are not one but two **pit prisons**. These were dark places from which the unfortunate prisoners seldom resurfaced. Dropped through a trap-door into almost total darkness, there was no possible means of escape.

The river side of the castle is particularly pleasant, with the trees overhanging the water and the castle's impressive walls towering above the grassy banks. To the left is a woodland walk beside the river.

> On leaving the castle, turn left onto the road and walk along for about 50 yards to the track on the left which winds its way towards the river. Continue along here to the bridge and once across the bridge turn right and follow the riverside path towards East Linton (whose name means 'settlement by the waterfall').
>
> After about $1\frac{1}{2}$ miles, pass under the A1 bridge, turn left at the cottage and walk up to the main road. Turn right onto Station Road, pass under the railway bridge, and turn left up Bridge Street. Continue straight on until you reach Preston Road (old signpost to Tyninghame, Whitekirk and North Berwick), and turn right for **Preston Mill (2)**. Continue until you reach the church, and walk down the path opposite that runs alongside the river.

At the start of this path is the site of St Baldred's Well - St Baldred founded

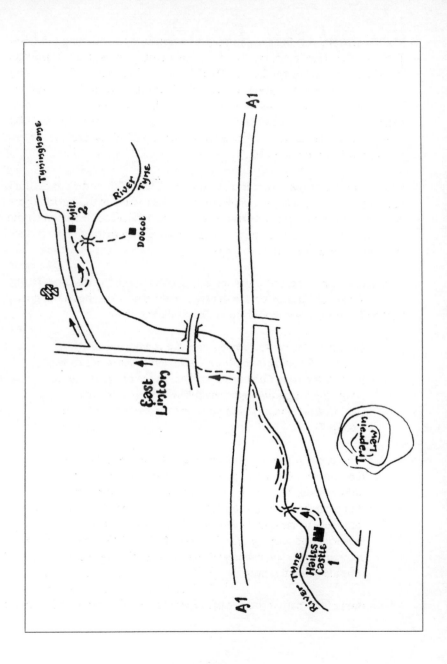

Tyninghame

Mill 2

River Tyne

Doocot

A1

East Linton

Traprain Law

A1

River Tyne

Hailes Castle 1

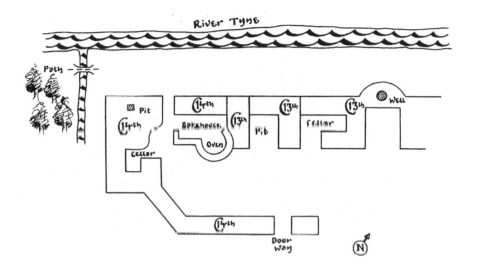

a settlement near Preston Mill in the 6th century.

> *Walk over the bridge and turn left for Preston Mill. Before you reach the mill, you will see the* **Phantassie Doocot** *(the name Phantassie means 'settlement by the water') up to the right.*

There has been a mill here for over 600 years, but the present **Preston Mill** only dates back 3-400 years. The waterwheel is a 19th century replacement. Flooding has always been a problem at Preston, and it finally brought about the closure of the mill as a commercial venture in 1948. Earlier floods, such as that of 1911, are marked by stones set in the wall at the level the water reached. After the 1948 flood, the mill was handed over to the National Trust who have preserved it as a working museum.

Preston Mill.

The interior of the mill with its complex and dangerous looking machinery is a stark contrast to the peaceful rural setting. Oats for both human and equine consumption were ground here after being dried in the extraordinarily roofed kiln house for anything between two hours and two days. The local farmers usually insisted that the oats be processed within a day in order to minimise the miller's opportunity to help himself to them. This problem arose because there was no way of quantifying exactly how much of the finished product could be made from any given amount of oats.

The duck pond outside is a haven for ducks and Muscovy geese, although in late summer the duckling population often incurs heavy losses form marauding crows.

Return to Hailes Castle by the same route.

17
The River Esk Walkway and Inveresk Garden

St Michaels Church
Riverside Walkway
Inveresk Garden

Opening Times
Inveresk Gardens open all year Mon-Fri 10am-4.30pm,
Sunday 2-5pm

Recommended Map
Ordnance Survey Landranger 66

Walking distance 1 mile

Directions to Start
A1 east from Edinburgh, then A199 to Musselburgh.
Follow the road to the left after crossing the bridge
over the River Esk, then turn right almost immediately
onto the A6124 towards Inveresk Garden. After the
road has turned sharp left and then sharp right, take
the next road to the right (at the end of the high
walls).

Starting Point: St Michaels Church (1)
OS Map Reference 344721

Inveresk Churchyard.

The massive and imposing **St Michaels Church** is not particularly attractive, but is notable for its memorials to a spectacularly unlucky military family. Just to the right of the path in front of the the church are the graves of the four sons of **Captain Ramsay**, whose second oldest son died on the Leeward Island Station in 1807 at the age of 19. His brother Alexander, the third son, died on the 1st January in 1815 in New Orleans at the age of 24. Then the eldest, Major William Norman Ramsay of the Royal Horse Artillery, fell at the Battle of Waterloo on the 18th June 1815 aged 33, having served for 16 years in Spain, Portugal, Egypt and France. The fourth son, Lieutenant David Ramsay RN completed the tragedy when he died the next month on the Jamaica Station in July 1815.

> *Walk along the path in front of the church and down to the*
> *riverside. The walkway along the river starts at the bridge in*
> *the centre of Musselburgh and stretches along the river to*
> *Whitecraig.*

*Turn left and walk along the River Esk to the next turning on
the left. At the top of the path turn right to Inveresk Garden.*

Inveresk Garden has a large variety of plants, and a guide can be
borrowed from the conservatory to the left of the entrance, which also has
some wicker chairs and a small aviary. Out in the garden, there is a quaint
rustic gazebo, some topiary and amongst the various trees are Himalayan
birch, walnut and sycamore.

*On leaving the garden, turn left and St Michaels Church is
straight along the road.*

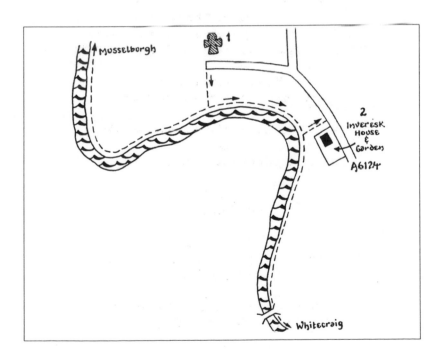

18
Dirleton Castle to Yellowcraigs

13th Century Castle
Gardens and Doocot
Gazebo
Picturesque Village

Opening Times
Dirleton Castle is open all year; summer Mon-Sat
9.30-7pm, Sun 2-7; winter Mon-Sat 9.30-4pm, Sun 2-4

Recommended Map
Ordnanace Survey Landranger Map 66

**Walking distance - 1 mile, but can be followed
by
Yellowcraigs Walk, a distance of 5 miles.**

Hotel
The Open Arms

Directions to Start
Follow A1 east from Edinburgh to the start of the
A198 which goes to Dirleton

**Starting Point: Dirleton Castle (1)
OS Map Reference 515840**

Dirleton Castle was originally constructed in the 13th century by the **De Vaux** family, Anglo-Normans who had come to Scotland in the 12th century. Consisting of a number of massive towers, the castle was held by the De Vaux's for about a century, until it passed by marriage to the **Halyburton** family. In the De Vaux period, the castle was besieged and captured for the first time during **Edward I's invasion of 1298**. It was held by the English until 1311. When the Halyburton's took over the castle in the mid 14th century, they set about repairing the damage done to the castle and extended the buildings to include a prison, pit and chapel. During their time the castle was visited by **James IV**. But the Halyburton male line also died out and the castle passed to the **Ruthvens**, later to be Earls of Gowrie, by marriage. The third Lord Ruthven was implicated in the murder of **David Rizzio**, Mary Queen of Scots Italian secretary, in 1566 in Holyroodhouse and the family's penchant for intrigue was continued by the fourth Lord Ruthven. He offered Dirleton Castle to Robert Logan of Restalrig as a bribe to secure his support in an attempt on **James VI**'s life. The plot against the king culminated in an assasination attempt in Perth on 6th August 1600. The plan was a disastrous failure; James VI survived while the Earl of Gowrie was killed. Gowrie's treachery resulted in the total ruination of the family, whose estates were confiscated and passed to the crown. In the next fifty years the castle passed through a number of hands and gained notoriety as the result of the imprisonment of witches in the castle in 1649. Many of them were strangled and burned at the stake, normal practise in the case of those accused of 'malefice' in the 17th century.

As with many other castles in the Lothians, Dirleton's power and influence disappeared virtually overnight with the appearance of **Cromwell**'s troops, and in particular his artillery, in 1650. At this time, the castle was held by Royalist 'Moss Troopers', one of whom, Patrick Gordon, was known as **'Steelhand the Mosser'**. In one encounter with Cromwellian troops he and his companions killed eight of them and threw another eight over a cliff into the sea. But on this occasion, they were quickly subdued after the fourth artillery shot killed one of the officers. They immediately surrendered to **General Monk** who responded by shooting a number of them and destroying the castle.

Enter the castle grounds by the main gate, and the gazebo is on your left. Walk up through the beautifully kept gardens to the staircase that leads up to the castle itself. At the top of the steps, the buidings to your right date from the 13th and 16th centuries, and those ahead from the 14th and 15th. Turn right and walk through to the oldest section of the castle, the De Vaux tower. The most impressive feature of this part of the castle is the Lord's Chamber in the south tower, with its vaulted roof and massive fireplace. It is interesting to note that the oldest part of the castle has survived the best. Continue up to the bee hive roof at the top of the tower from which you can look down on the drawbridge and moat.

Return to the courtyard and the stairs to the right lead up to **the Great Hall** built by the Ruthven's in the 16th century.

Return to the courtyard again and the main castle entrance is on the right. Above the passage that leads onto the drawbridge you can see the **'murder hole'** which was used to provide unwelcome guests with fatal surprises.

The next exit from the courtyard leads through the bakehouse and the vaults to the **chapel**, which has two alcoves beside the fireplace which show signs of decoration. Below the chapel is the **prison and the pit**. The pit is only eleven feet square and is in total darkness. This is where the Dirleton witches would have been held.

Above the Vaults is the Great Hall of the **Halyburton** period which retains little of its former splendour although the **carved stone buffet**, which was used to show the family silver, still displays the Halyburton coat of arms.

In the grounds of the castle is the best dovecot in East Lothian. It was built by the Ruthvens in the 16th century.

Walk out of the castle and over to the village green. Passing the Castle Inn

Dirleton Churchyard.
17th C Tomb.

on the left and the war memorial on your right, you come to **the church (2)**, the churchyard of which has a number of interesting 17th century gravestones.

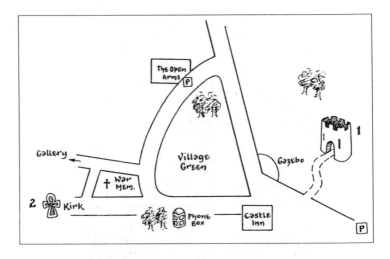

Walk past the Open Arms Hotel, and turn left down to Yellowcraigs Beach about a mile further on. Once at the beach, the island of Fidra, is straight ahead. This end of the island is known as the South Dog and the far end, where the lighthouse stands, is the North Dog.

This beach was one of the locations used in Stevenson's novel *Catriona*.

Walk down to the left, past the fenced off Marine Villa and the World War Two gun emplacement and along the beach to the caves. Either return by the same route to the village, or alternatively continue along the top of the cliffs to Gullane Bay about a mile away.

Fidra.

Here is no dwelling of man, and scarce any passage, or at most of vagabond children running at their play. Gillane is a small place on the far side of the Ness, the folk of Dirleton go to their business in the inland fields, and those of North Berwick straight to the sea fishing from their haven; so that few parts of the coast are lonlier. But I mind, as we crawled upon our bellies into that multiplicity of heights and hollows, keeping a bright eye upon all sides, and our hearts hammering at our ribs, there was such a shining of the sun and the sea, such a stir of wind in the bent grass, and such a bustle of down-popping rabbits and up-flying gulls, that the desert seemed to me like a place alive. No doubt it was in all ways well chosen for a secret embarkation, if the secret had been kept; and even now that it was out, and the place watched, we were able to creep unpercieved to the front of the sand hills, where they look down immediately on the beach and sea.

From *Catriona* by **Robert Louis Stevenson**

19
Tantallon Castle to Scoughall Beach

Whitekirk
Tantallon Castle
Bass Rock
Scoughall Beach

Opening times
Tantallon Castle open all year; summer Mon-Sat 9.30-
7pm, Sun 2-7; winter Mon-Sat 9.30-4pm, Sun 2-4pm,
closed Thurs pm and all day Friday

Recommended Map
Ordnance Survey Landranger 67

Walking distance 3 miles

Direction to Start
A1 east from Edinburgh. Once through East Linton,
turn left onto the A198. Before you reach Tantallon,
stop off at Whitekirk.

Starting Point: Tantallon Castle (1)
OS Map Reference 851596

Whitekirk village has a historic and beautiful old kirk, St Mary's, built from red sandstone and dating from the 14th century. This has been a place of Christian worship since early times - St Baldred may have founded a church here in the 6th century - and pilgrims came from far and wide to visit the holy well which stood close by, although the exact site of the well remains a mystery. In the 15th century, this tiny rural hamlet must have seemed extremely busy: in 1413, 15,653 pilgrims visited Whitekirk, **James IV** and Aeneas Sylvius Piccolomini, later **Pope Pius II**, both made pilgrimages to Whitekirk It is said that as a result of walking the ten miles from the coast barefoot through the snow, Piccolimini was plagued by ill health for the rest of his life.

In 1650, during the siege of **Tantallon Castle**, General Monk stabled his horses in the church.

On the 26th February 1914 the church was severely damaged in a bizarre suffragette protest against the rough treatment they were receiving at the hands of the authorities. At around the same time they blew up Lloyd George's house amongst other things. The church was later rebuilt under the guidance of Sir Robert Lorimer.

The interior of the church is surprisingly large and has echoing acoustics. High up on the wall at the far end, a small section of blackened masonry remains as a visible sign of the 1914 fire.

Once outside, the most unusual feature on the north side of the church is the small carved head set high up in the wall. Its origins are unknown.

Over the wall on the north side of the churchyard is the mediaeval **Tithe Barn**, one the few remaining in Scotland. In medieval times, the church was entitled to one tenth of the crops of all the local inhabitants, hence the term 'tithe', and these would be deposited in the tithe barn.

Tantallon Castle was built in the middle of the 14th century by **Sir William Douglas**, whose association with Robert the Bruce took him from relative obscurity to being first Earl of Douglas. The sheer size of the castle he founded reflects the family's meteoric rise. However, his descendents split into two feuding factions, the Red and the Black Douglases, and it was the Red Douglases who held Tantallon. Perhaps the

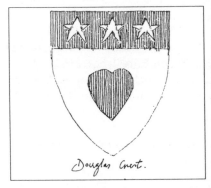

Douglas Crest.

most famous of the Red Douglases was the fifth Earl, Archibald, who earned the nickname **'Bell-the-Cat'** because he was the only member of the nobility to oppose James IV. This action led to him being besieged by the king at Tantallon in 1491, but a negotiated settlement was reached. Bell-the-Cat eventually died peacefully at Tantallon, although the same could not be said for his unfortunate heirs: both his sons, William and George, were killed with their king at the **battle of Flodden** in 1513. The castle was to be the scene of another siege in 1528 when **James V**, who had been held prisoner for three years by the sixth Earl, arrived to take his revenge. The castle withstood a long bombardment until the siege ended after twenty days when the kings artillery ran out of gunpowder. Within a year the sixth Earl had fled abroad and the castle passed to the crown. It was not until James V's death in 1542 that he was able to return to Tantallon. During the Rough Wooing, Tantallon was one of the few castles to escape the attentions of the English forces because the sixth Earl aligned himself with Henry VIII. By the mid-1550's the castle passed back to the Crown. The final siege of Tantallon took place in 1651 when the castle was defended by only thirty **Moss Troopers**. Their efficient guerilla actions against Cromwell's troops had made them a threat that could not be ignored. After a barrage lasting twelve days, the castle was devastated and the Moss Troopers led by Captain Alexander Setton attempted to surrender.

> "They presently beat a parley, but it would not be heard; then they hung out a little clout; after they hung out a great sheet our men shot at it; at last the Governor came upon the walls and entreated he might be heard."
> *Contemporary English account.*

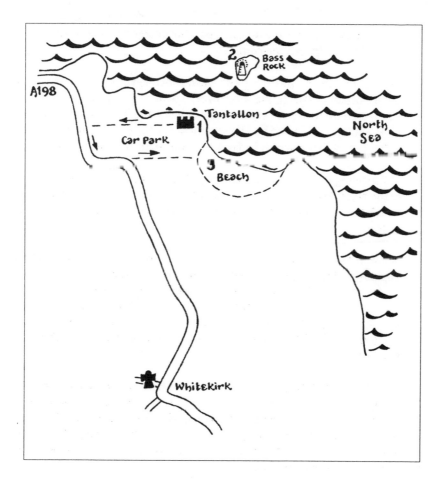

The surrender was accepted and the Moss Troopers were led away to English prisons.

By the end of the 17th century, the castle was no more than a ruin.

As you approach the castle from the south west, you will see a network of ditches and earthworks. These were intended to prevent attacking forces from bringing their artillery close to the castle walls.

Walk through the outer gate, past the doocot and across the drawbridge into the castle.

This central tower was the most heavily fortified part of the castle, the outer section of which, the foretower, was added in the 16th century to strengthen the tower's resistance to artillery attack. Through the tower is the courtyard. Lean-to buildings would once have occupied much of this area - but all that remains today is the **hundred foot deep well**.

On entering the courtyard, the **Hall Block** is on the left. This is the site of the Great Hall and much of the accomodation of the castle. At the west end of the Hall Block is the **Douglas Tower** below which is the grim pit prison.

Approaching the castle the Curtain Wall, although imposing, gives no impression of the labyrinthine interior. A number of narrow stairways lead to the extensive battlements and give access to the towers. Going up the stairs, you will notice a number of rooms full of rubble. This was done to provide extra protection against artillery. High up on the exposed and windswept walls there are excellent views of East Lothian and the **Bass Rock (2)**.

In 1691 four Jacobite prisoners held in the **Bass Rock castle** overpowered their captors. Apparently aided by pirates, they astonishingly held out for four years before lack of food compelled them to surrender. They had survived on a diet of fish and gannets, the gannets being caught by devious means: a herring was attached to a wooden board and when the bird dived for the fish, its beak stuck in the board.

Leaving the castle, walk back to the main road and turn left. Continue up to Auldhame Farm and carry on down the single track road. After half a mile there is an automatic barrier (50 pence for drivers) which leads on to the car park and a **delightful sandy cove (3).**

Return to the start by the same route.

20
North Berwick Law

Iron Age Remains
Hill Fort
Whale Bone Jaws
Glacial Crag and Tail

Recommended Map
Ordnance Survey Landranger 66

Distance 1 mile

Directions to Start
A1 east from Edinburgh. Once past East Linton, turn
left at the A198 and up past Whitekirk and Tantallon
Castle to North Berwick. Turn left at the B1347 to the
car park at North Berwick Law.

**Starting Point North Berwick Law car park (1)
OS Map Reference 555842**

North Berwick Law is one of the most striking landmarks in the East Lothian countryside. At 614 ft, it dominates the flat landscape despite its relatively modest size. This is a classic **crag and tail** remnant from the last Ice Age. Like Edinburgh Castle rock and Arthurs Seat, it is a volcanic plug of hard basaltic rock which resisted the advancing ice. The result was that the glacier was forced over the top and round the side of the hard rock leaving the tail on the other side and the hill as it is today.

For many centuries this was a natural defensive site and was occupied from the iron age to the middle ages. About fifty feet below the summit, the remains of an ancient hill fort are visible. In more recent times the hill has been used as a lookout post, in both the Napoleonic Wars and the two World Wars. The summit is marked by a set of **whale's jaw bones** dating from 1936.

Walking up the hill, you will see the remains of Iron Age burial sites, also look out for the wildlife that now inhabits the hill - green woodpecker, red shank, wren and snipe.

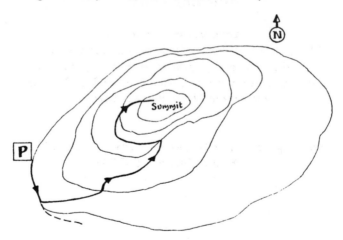

*From the top of the hill there are excellent views of the coastline, the **Bass Rock** and **Tantallon Castle.***

21
House of the Binns to Blackness Castle

House of the Binns
The Dalyell family
The Folly
Blackness Castle

Opening Times
House of the Binns open Easter weekend and May 1 to
Sept 30, 2-5pm except Friday. Woodland walk open all
year 10-7. No dogs allowed.
Blackness Castle open summer Mon-Sat 9.30-7pm, Sun
2-7; winter Mon-Sat 9.30-4pm, Sun 2-4pm, closed
Thurs pm and all day Friday

Recommended Map
Ordnance Survey Landranger 65

Distance 4 miles

Directions to Start
A90 west from Edinburgh to Forth Road Bridge. Just
before the bridge turn left on to the A904 and continue for about 4 miles to the House of the Binns.

Starting Point House of the Binns (1)
OS Map Reference 051786

The House of the Binns is the home of the Dalyell family who have lived there since the house was built by **Thomas Dalyell**, a successful Edinburgh merchant, in the 1620's. The exterior of the house is a more recent 19th century addition. By far the most famous member of the family was **General Thomas 'Tam' Dalyell** (1599-1685) who enjoyed one of the most wide ranging military careers of the 17th century. Always a loyal supporter of the crown, he fought for Charles I in the English Civil War and was captured at the **Battle of Worcester in 1651**. He was imprisoned in the Tower of London but managed to escape and fled into exile. After the execution of Charles I, Tam vowed never to cut his hair or beard again until the monarchy was restored. The future king, Charles II, who always addressed Tam as "your affectionate friend", arranged for him to go to Moscow to serve **Czar Alexis Michaelovitch**, the father of Peter the Great. In Russia Tam became a general in the Imperial army and loyally served the Czar for ten years, during which time he developed camoflage, before returning to Britain in the 1660's after the restoration of Charles II. One legacy of his service in Russia was his introduction of the thumbscrew, or 'thumbykins', to Scotland.

Tam Dalyell was a well educated, complex individual with a wry sense of humour. On one of his regular visits to the court of Charles II, the King commented on his unkempt appearance and unfashionable attire. The next time he visited the King, Tam appeared dressed in the height of contemporary fashion, much to the amusement of the monarch who recognised the irony of this gesture.

Tam continued his military career at home, leading Charles II's forces against the Covenanters during the **Pentland Rising**. His involvement in the **Battle of Rullion Green** in 1666 (see Walk 2) and the subsequent savage persecution of the Covenanters - more than thirty of whom were hanged - earned him their undying hatred. They called him **'The Bluidie Muscovite'** and spread rumours that he was in league with the devil. This was not entirely fair, as Tam was not responsible for the persecution that followed the battle and resigned in protest at the excesses of his colleagues. Before the battle, Tam had promised safe conduct for the covenanters camp followers, but after the battle many of them were taken to Edinburgh and shot. Even in his old age, Tam remained active, and in 1682 he founded the Scots Greys.

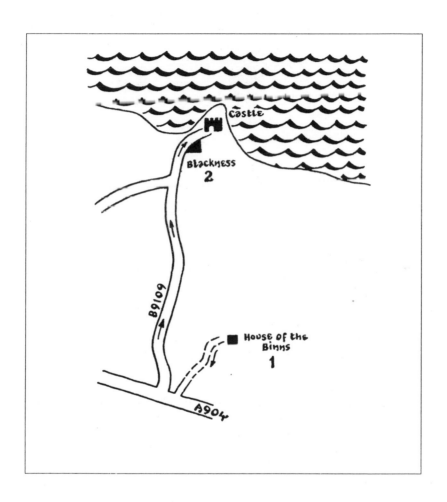

Castle

Blackness

2

B9109

House of the Binns

1

A904

The House of the Binns.

The House of the Binns (meaning hills) is currently the home of the well known Labour MP for Linlithgow, **Tam Dalyell**, although since 1944 it has been in the care of the National Trust for Scotland.

Inside the house, the first room is the main hall which has a number of interesting family heirlooms. On the wall to the left of the fireplace is an ornate gilded cutlass which was given to a member of the family to commemorate his bravery during a naval action in which was severly wounded. Different swords were presented for varying degrees of bravery - this is a fifty guinea sword, the second most expensive. Just to the right of the main entrance is a **marble table**. It is said that during the 1660's Tam Dalyell would sit at this table by the pond in the garden and play cards with the Devil himself. On one occasion Tam is said to have won, whereupon the devil overturned the table and threw it into the pond. It was recovered from the pond earlier this century and evidence of its diabolical associations can be seen in the hoof-shaped mark on one corner of the table.

On the way through to the next room, there is a door on the left which conceals a **secret passageway** to Blackness Castle.

In the main dining room there are portraits of **General Tam Dalyell** and other members of the family, such as **James Dalyell** who was scalped by Red Indians in 1763 and **Captain Dalyell** who was killed at sea in 1765 during the **Seven Years War**. Dominating the room are the black leather boots worn by Tam Dalyell in Russia. There are a number of unlikely stories connected with these boots. On one occasion a member of the family took them with him when he moved away from Binns and the boots are said to have walked back on their own. The Covenanters claimed, after Tam's death, that if water was poured into the boots it would immediatly boil, as their late owner was himself now burning in the fires of Hell.

Upstairs on the first floor you will see a number of rooms that were extensively redecorated in preparation for the visit of **King Charles I**. An expert Italian plasterer was commissioned to carry out the work and his elaborate ceiling designs have survived intact in the Great Hall and the King's Rooms. Unfortunately, the king's visit never took place.

Outside the house, take the path to the right through the trees. This leads to the **folly** which was built in 1826 by **Sir James Dalyell** in order to win a bet. The winner of the bet was to be the person who could build the cheapest folly. With this rather uninteresting tower, Sir James won.

Walk down to the A904 and turn right and then right again onto the B9109. At the junction, turn right and walk down to the village of Blackness. The road that follows the coast to the right leads to Blackness Castle.

Blackness Castle (2) dates from the 15th century and its main function was as a state prison. Unlike so many other castles in the area, it has remained virtually intact having been continuously occupied until the start of this century. The **Crichton** family, who also held Crichton Castle (see Walk 8), built the original castle as a typical fortified tower enclosed by a defensive wall. After the 1450's Blackness was in Royal hands and was being used as a prison to hold important people such as **Cardinal Beaton**. It was also being transformed into a massive artillery fortification in an attempt to keep pace with ever increasing threat that the introduction of gunpowder brought with it. However, it was to be a hundred years before

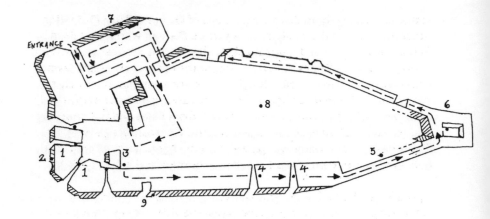

1 Gunholes
2 Great Hall
3 Stairs
4 East Wall
5 Original Wall
6 Pit and Prison
7 Spur
8 Central Tower
9 Original Castle Entrance

the castle was seriously threatened. All the work of the previous century was to prove futile in the face of Cromwell's all-conquering artillery, although it is said that the castle's capture owed more to the shadowy treachery of the Lord Clerk Register, **Major Johnston of Wariston**, than to Cromwell's guns. Its years as an impregnable fortress were over, and after this the castle was simply used as a prison and, in the 19th century, an ammunition dump.

Approaching the castle, you will see a number of buildings outside the walls. These are mostly barracks dating from the 19th century. The most striking external features are the massive oval gunholes in the south tower, and the lighter coloured stonework to the right of these betrays the damage done by **Cromwell**'s army in 1650. On the east wall, just past the south tower, you can still see the remains of the original entrance. Return to the darkly oppresive entrance in the south west corner of the castle and go into the bleak, rough-hewn courtyard with its forbidding central tower. It was in this tower that most of the prisoners were held.

Turning right and into the south tower you can see the enormous thickness of the walls and the gun positions that were added in the 16th century. There are a variety of empty rooms which lead off the stairway up to **the Great Hall.**

Leave the south tower and walk up the steps onto the east wall. At the northernmost point there is a small tower which was also used as a prison. From this room, prisoners were dropped through a trap door into **the pit** below. This must have been one of the worst places of confinement in Scotland, with the sea partially flooding the pit twice a day to add to the prisoner's misery.

Walk along the west wall to the spur at the south west corner of the castle. This is yet another 16th century addition whose gun positions were intended to make the castle entrance invulnerable.

On leaving the castle, return to the House of the Binns along the same route.

22
Dalmeny House to South Queensferry and Dalmeny Village

Dalmeny House
Firth of Forth
Forth Rail Bridge
Hawes Pier
Dalmeny Church

Opening Times
Dalmeny House open Sunday-Thursday, May-September, 2-5.30pm
Walkway to South Queensferry closed on Fridays

Recommended Map
Ordnance Survey Landranger 65

Walking distance 5 miles

Tearoom
Dalmeny House

Directions to Start
A90 towards Forth Road Bridge to B924. Dalmeny House is off the B924 to the right.

Starting Point Dalmeny House (1)
OS Map Ref 168780

Dalmeny House replaced **Barnbougle Castle** as the Primrose family home in 1817. The Primroses had lived at Barnbougle since the 1660's when it was bought by **Sir Archibald Primrose**. Sir Archibald's loyalty to the Royalist cause eventually led to his rise to prominence as the foremost legal officer of the Crown in Scotland, and his son was to be the first Viscount Rosebery. His descendents were content to live in the draughty Barnbougle Castle for 150 years until the fourth Earl of Rosebery built the new house.

The most famous member of the Rosebery family was the **fifth Earl** (1847-1929), also called Archibald, who had succeeded his father when he was twenty. In 1878 he married the heiress Hannah Rothschild. The fifth Earl was to play a major part in public life as a leading figure in the Liberal Party: under Gladstone he served as Foreign Secretary before briefly becoming **Prime Minister** in 1894.

"It is beginning to be hinted that we are a nation of amateurs"
Lord Rosebery's *Rectorial Address*
Glasgow University, 16th April 1900

Approaching the house, the most successful feature of this **Tudor Gothic** design is the roofscape with its multiplicity of chimneys, turrets and ornamentation. In front of the house is a life size statue of the thoroughbred racehorse *King Tom* which was brought from the Rothschild's house at Mentmore.

Inside Dalmeny House, the main hall features a number of portraits and a collection of rare Spanish tapestries designed by **Goya** at the turn of the 19th century. The elaborate ceiling appears to be made of wood, but much of it is in fact cunningly concealed plasterwork. The main staircase leads to the apartments used by the family.

The house features a delightful library with commanding views over the lawns to the Firth of Forth. This room, with its fine **Joshua Reynolds** portrait of Rockingham over the fireplace, is still used by the family. Beside the library is the drawing room which is now used to display some of the Mentmore treasures, including a porcelain dog belonging to **Marie Antoinette** and some drab French tapestries, brought into the family by the marriage of Hannah Rothschild to the fifth Earl.

In the Gothic Corridor there is an enormous penknife brought from Barnbougle, a sea chest which belonged to Captain Cook and the Ramshead snuff box given by James VI to the Sheep Heid Inn at Duddingston **(see Edinburgh Walks Volume One, Walk 9)**.

Just off this corridor is the **Napoleon Room** which houses the fifth Earl's collection of Napoleonic memorabilia - including a striking portrait of Napoleon as a young man at the **Battle of Lodi**, his desk from St Helena, and the **Duke of Wellington**'s campaign chair. There is also the original sketch made by the painter **David** for his celebrated painting of Napoleon's Imperial Coronation. The coronation ceremony was to be performed by the Pope, but at the last moment Napoleon siezed the crown and placed it on his own head.

Tea is served in the **Dining Room** which overlooks the Forth and contains a number of portraits. Of particular interest are those of George Selwyn - a clear case of dog/owner versimilitude, and **Edward Gibbon**, the 18th century historian and author of *The Decline and Fall of the Roman Empire*, who bears a striking resemblance to the comedian **Mel Smith.**

Back across the entrance hall there are a series of rooms which include the **Garden Hall** with its bust of the tragic son of Napoleon III. He was serving as a junior officer with the British Army in Southern Africa in 1879 when he and a companion were ambushed by Zulu warriors. His companion escaped, but the Prince was cut to pieces.

Through the Garden Hall is a small exhibition of plans and designs relating to the construction of Dalmeny House and the **Robert Adam** plans to extend Barnbougle Castle which were never executed.

Outside the house, turn left past 'King Tom' and walk down by the golf course to the road. This leads past **Barnbougle Castle (2)**, which is private, and round the coast to the Forth Bridges and **Hawes Pier (3)** via Hound Point, a distance of about 2 miles.

The Forth Rail Bridge is over a mile long and was built by Sir John Fowler and Benjamin Baker between 1883 and 1890 at a cost of two and three quarter million pounds. The design of the bridge allows for an expansion of over three feet during the summer. On the left is the **Hawes Inn** which features in *Kidnapped* by **Robert Louis Stevenson.**

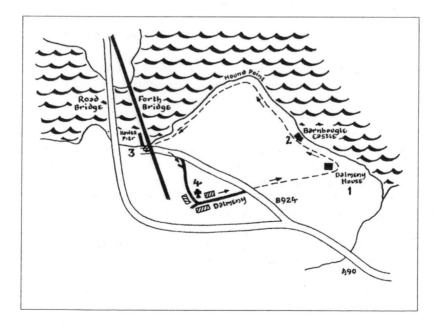

...the neighbourhood of the inn looked pretty lonely at that time of day, for the boat had just gone north with passengers. A skiff, however, lay beside the pier, with some seamen sleeping on the thwarts; this, as Ransome told me, was the brig's boat waiting for the Captain; and about half a mile off, and all alone in the anchorage, he showed me The Covenant herself. There was a seagoing bustle on board; yards were swinging into place; and as the wind blew from that quarter, I could hear the song of the sailors as they pulled upon the ropes. After all I had listened to upon the way, I looked at that ship with an extreme abhorrence; and from the bottom of my heart I pitied all poor souls that were condemned to sail in her.

From *Kidnapped* by **Robert Louis Stevenson**

Walk back under the Rail Bridge and follow the main road (B924) to the first turn on the right. Turn right and walk up to Dalmeny Village. Turn left at the junction and the fine Norman church is on the left.

Dalmeny Church has an elaborate Romanesque doorway that features a number of interlocking arches above the main door. The symbolic carvings over the door include mythological creatures and human heads. The interior features some fine 12th century vaulting and outside, close to the door is an unusual stone coffin.

Continue down the road, across the B924 and back to the starting point at Dalmeny House.

23
Ratho and the Union Canal

Ratho Parish Church
The Union Canal
Canal Boats

Ratho Canal Centre 031-333 1320/1251

Recommended Map
Ordnance Survey Landranger 65

Directions to Start
A8 to Newbridge roundabout. Take the second exit
from the roundabout, and then turn left and left again
for Ratho Village, about a mile further on.

Starting Point Ratho Parish Church
OS Map Ref 140709

Ratho Church was originally built in the 13th century, but much of the present building is 18th century. The gable ends are the oldest part of the church as can be seen from the deep groove worn by the bell chain over the years. The churchyard contains a number of unusual tombstones, the most interesting of which is the **stone coffin** just outside the church door. Elaborately carved to represent wood panelling and brass handles - the underside of the coffin is particularly curious - it commemorates the death of William Mitchell, a preacher:

> who suffered an instantaneous death by strok from a thrashing machin on the farm of Graysmill 4th Dec 1809. His worth endeared him to his freinds and his talent rendered him the ornament of his family.

Walk up to the canal.

The Union Canal was opened in 1822 and linked up to the Forth and Clyde Canal. It carried goods and passengers, and on a good day, with frequent changes of horses, the journey between Edinburgh and Glasgow could be completed in 7 hours. The canal's working life was abruptly terminated in 1842 with the opening of the railway.

From the bridge, a short walk to the west takes you to the Lin's Mill aquaduct over the River Almond, which has five spans supporting a cast iron channel. It is possible to extend this walk considerably by continuing along the towpath to Linlithgow, a distance of about 12 miles.

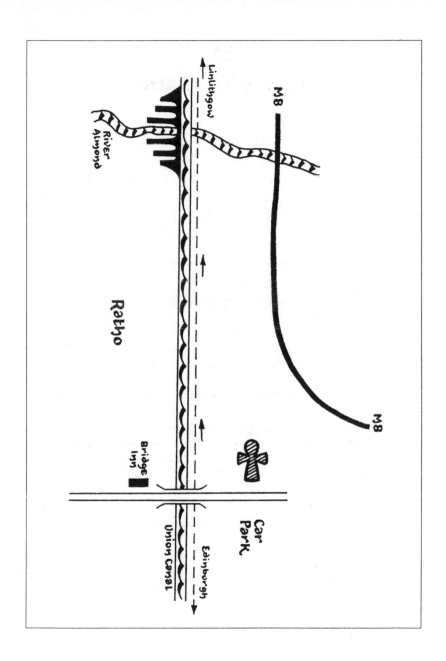

24
Inchcolm Island

Inchcolm Abbey
Chapter House
First and Second World War Fortifications
Hermit's Cell
Hog Back Stone

Opening Times
Phone 031-331 1454 for details of sailings on The Maid
of the Forth, which are usually between May and
September.
There is a charge of £1.20 for visitors who take their
own boat to Inchcolm.

Walking Distance 1 mile

Directions to Start
A90 towards the Forth Road Bridge. Turn off the dual
carriageway onto the B924 to Queensferry. The
departure point is just on the other side of the Forth
Rail Bridge.

Starting Point Hawes Pier

The trip from **Hawes Pier** takes 1/2 an hour and provides excellent views of the **Forth Bridges, Inch Garvie, and Barnbougle Castle**.

Inchcolm is one of the four Inches, or islands, of the Forth. The others are **Inch Garvie, Inchmickery** and **Inchkeith**. The island has been a place of religious significance since early times and it takes its name from **St Colm**. Inchcolm was originally inhabited by hermits, and just to the north of the abbey is a small building which may have been a **hermit's cell**. The abbey itself was founded in the mid 12th century as a result of a promise made by **Alexander I**. The hermits had given him shelter when he was stranded on the island, and in return he undertook to establish a monastery. The king died before this could be accomplished, but by the end of the 12th century building had begun and Augustinian Canons were in residence. At the start of the 13th century the Priory's importance was such that Bishops were being buried within its walls. By the middle of the 13th century it had become an abbey. The abbey survived the ravages of war in the 14th century, when it was constantly attacked and plundered by the English, and building continued right up to the Reformation. In the 16th century further English attacks and the onset of the Reformation ended hundreds of years of worship on the island.

After landing on the island, head to the left past the shop and up the hill to the **fortifications (1)**.

Before you get to the top of the hill, walk through the **tunnel** that passes through the hill. This was built by the Royal Engineers between 1916 and 1917 to allow quicker access to the gun positions on the other side. During the First World War, Inchcolm and the other islands of the Forth were fortified to protect the naval anchorage that lay to west of the Forth Bridge. On Inchcolm itself, the remains of the naval gun positions can still be seen at this end of the island. The island was also garrisoned during the Second World War, but its guns were never fired in action. The roofs of the concrete fortifications were camoflaged by having rocks embedded in the concrete, and this can still be seen today.

Walk down the hill to the **abbey buildings (2)**.

Inchcolm Abbey is a well preserved though complex ruin. The central feature of the monastic buildings is the 13th century **Chapter House**, where the Abbot, Prior and Sub-Prior presided over the administration of the monastery. With its Romanesque doorway and well preserved vaulting, it is one of the finest in Scotland. The surrounding Cloister, although much altered in the later Middle Ages, has also survived intact.

To the north of the **Cloister** are to be found the remains of the first Abbey Church and to the east the second church, probably dating from the 15th century. Amongst the ruins of the second church are the remains of a section of mediaeval church painting.

The upper storeys of many of the other buildings can still be reached by means of a number of diminutive staircases. Much smaller than the staircases of many of the mainland's ruins, they highlight the compact size of mediaeval monks. Above the south side of the Cloister is the **Refectory**, which has a raised pulpit at the far window where one of the monks would have read appropriate sections of the Bible during meals. At the north side of the Cloister one of the staircases gives access to the tower from which the whole of the Abbey and the island can be viewed.

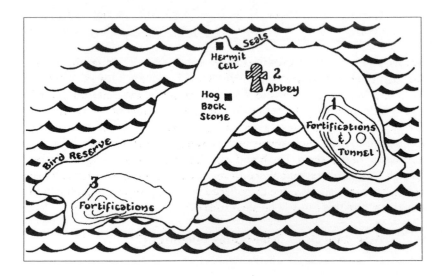

Chapter House, Inchcolm .

*Leaving the Abbey, walk past the Hermit's Cell with its stone roof, and up to the **Hog Back Stone**.*

Possibly dating from the 10th century, it has been suggested that the stone was the memorial of a **Viking warrior**. Its typically Scandinavian decoration adds weight to this theory.

The path continues past the concrete foundations of the 4.7 inch guns that stood here and on to the west end of the island which is a **bird sanctuary**. Inchcolm Island is also the home of a thriving **seal colony**.

Notes